T0323948

This book is very timely given the deep division in how Americans view our political system and how much or how little they value people who work in political environments. Civil service systems have long protected government employees, who at times, work in highly charged political environments. Dr. Kellough explores the evolution of the federal civil service system and reforms over the past few years as he traces the partisan effort to dismantle the federal workforce.

Doug Goodman, Professor of Public Administration,
University of Central Florida

THE FRAGILITY OF MERIT

While the operation and structure of the public workforce is not a matter that is on the minds of most, the consequences for the nature and effectiveness of government are substantial. *The Fragility of Merit* provides a detailed examination of the importance of a professionally competent and politically neutral public service.

Illustrating the fundamental fragility of the federal civil service in the United States and the underlying concept of merit in public employment, J. Edward Kellough demonstrates how a particular view of presidential power grounded in unitary executive theory was used during Donald J. Trump's term in office. Specifically, he reviews various efforts to subordinate the public workforce to presidential authority and explains how those actions threatened to undermine bureaucratic expertise that is desperately needed in government.

The Fragility of Merit makes a persuasive case for protecting the civil service and for rebuilding a national consensus in favor of merit in public employment. It will benefit researchers, academics, students, and others with an interest in public administration, public personnel management, government, and bureaucracy.

J. Edward Kellough is the Thomas P. and M. Jean Lauth Professor of Public Affairs at the University of Georgia where he serves as Head of the Department of Public Administration and Policy. Dr. Kellough specializes primarily in the field of public-sector human resources management. He is an elected Fellow of the National Academy of Public Administration, has served as President of the Network of Schools of Public Policy, Affairs, and Administration (NASPAA), and has served as Chair of the Section on Public Administration of the American Political Science Association and as Chair of the American Society for Public Administration, Section of Personnel and Labor Relations and the Section on Public Administration Education.

THE FRAGILITY OF MERIT

Presidential Power and the Civil Service Under Trump

J. Edward Kellough

Routledge
Taylor & Francis Group

NEW YORK AND LONDON

Designed cover image: B Christopher/Alamy Stock Photo

First published 2025
by Routledge
605 Third Avenue, New York, NY 10158

and by Routledge
4 Park Square, Milton Park, Abingdon, Oxon, OX14 4RN

Routledge is an imprint of the Taylor & Francis Group, an informa business

Library of Congress Cataloging-in-Publication Data
Names: Kellough, J. Edward, author.
Title: The fragility of merit : presidential power and the civil service
under Trump / J. Edward Kellough.
Description: New York, NY : Routledge, 2025. | Includes bibliographical
references and index. |
Identifiers: LCCN 2024030661 (print) | LCCN 2024030662 (ebook) | ISBN
9781032656373 (hardback) | ISBN 9781032656342 (paperback) | ISBN
9781032656380 (ebook)
Subjects: LCSH: United States. Merit Systems Protection Board | United
States. Office of Personnel Management. | United States. Federal Labor
Relations Authority. | Civil service reform--United States. | United
States--Politics and government--2017-2021.
Classification: LCC JK681 .K45 2025 (print) | LCC JK681 (ebook) | DDC
352.6/30973--dc23/eng/20240923
LC record available at https://lccn.loc.gov/2024030661
LC ebook record available at https://lccn.loc.gov/2024030662

ISBN: 978-1-032-65637-3 (hbk)
ISBN: 978-1-032-65634-2 (pbk)
ISBN: 978-1-032-65638-0 (ebk)

DOI: 10.4324/9781032656380

Typeset in Times New Roman
by KnowledgeWorks Global Ltd.

CONTENTS

PREFACE AND ACKNOWLEDGMENTS

The work of government is labor intensive. The men and women employed in the various departments and agencies of government are responsible for translating policy directives from legislative mandates into the day-to-day operations of public programs. They are the key to effective public service. They are answerable to the President and the Congress and are supervised by political appointees who sit atop their organizations. They operate within the confines of law interpreted by the courts and, ultimately, the U.S. Supreme Court. They are subject to public scrutiny as well as to professional norms and the rules of ethics.

Collectively, these forces operate to constrain actions available to government agencies and their employees. The bureaucracy, in short, works within the boundaries set by legislation and political and public scrutiny. However, within those constraints, there is always a range of options available to bureaucrats responsible for policy implementation who must respond to circumstances and issues unforeseen when programs are initially authorized. Over many decades, as the government has been called upon to address increasingly complex problems, the system by which bureaucratic officials are employed has stressed selection based on demonstrated expertise to guide their exercise of discretion. That system has also shielded those employees from political manipulation. This structure, known generally as the merit system, is the foundation for the public workforce. It works to ensure that employment is based upon competence exercised in a politically neutral fashion.

There can be no question that the merit system constrains political control. That is its purpose. It does not eliminate political control, but it does limit it.

As a result, this system poses a dilemma for political accountability. The President, for example, has constitutional authority to exercise "executive power" (Article II, Section 1) and to "take Care that the Laws be faithfully executed" (Article II, Section 3). These constitutional provisions, plus the President's appointment authority specified in Article II, Section 2 of the Constitution, give the President enormous executive authority. The initial establishment of the federal merit system through the Pendleton Act of 1883 recognized that authority, as did President Carter's significant federal civil service reforms in 1978. Indeed, the successful operation of the federal merit system requires presidential support. As noted in the following pages, the merit system for the federal civil service "presumes the presence of a President who understands and is committed to the concept of merit and has the political will to secure its preservation" (Chapter 1, infra).

Given the structure of the merit system and the constitutional basis of presidential authority, what should a President do when bureaucratic decisions regarding policy run counter to the President's priorities? Generally, there are two options. One would be to seek legislation to change the bureaucratic mandate. Virtually all federal programs are authorized by and funded by Congress.[1] If a President is unhappy with the direction of a federal policy or program, he/she could seek legislation amending that policy or program. However, given the political party composition of Congress, such legislation may be difficult or impossible to obtain. In that case, a second option would be to exert greater presidential control over the bureaucracy and the operation of merit in employment.

This second option for altering the course of the federal bureaucracy was pursued by President Trump and his Administration from 2017 to 2021. Indeed, conservative supporters of the former President are now, as he is campaigning for reelection in 2024, pushing the same agenda. In the early summer of 2024, the former President and his aids claimed that the President had the authority, for example, to impound or refuse to spend money appropriated by Congress for programs that the President disfavors (Stein and Bogage, 2024). Trump reportedly claimed the "authority to cease programs altogether, even if lawmakers fund them" (Stein and Bogage, 2024). Trump and his supporters have also promised to reimplement and strengthen his policies regarding the federal civil service that were in place during his Presidency.

Those Trump policies to weaken the federal merit system and strengthen presidential control of the bureaucracy are the subject of this book. They included (1) an effort to disable the federal Merit Systems Protection Board, the agency that hears appeals from federal employees of prohibited personnel practices;

(2) a series of Executive Orders from 2018 to weaken federal employee unions and make it easier to fire federal workers; (3) an effort to dismantle the U.S. Office of Personnel Management and place responsibility for personnel policy in the Executive Office of the President; (4) the transfer of tens of thousands of federal employees with policy responsibility from the federal Competitive Service into a new category in the Excepted Service where they could be much more easily dismissed and vacancies could be filled non-competitively; and (5) the implementation of policies by the Federal Labor Relations Authority, the agency established to protect and oversee federal collective bargaining, that reversed decades of precedent to disfavor federal employee unions. Familiarity with the details of these actions is needed to fully understand the threat they posed to the federal merit system, and those details are provided in subsequent pages. Taken together, these actions during the Trump Presidency fully illustrate the fragility of merit.

Several people have assisted me as I worked on this project, and I have learned much through my conversations with them. All errors of fact or interpretation that remain are, of course, mine alone. First, I wish to thank my wife, Vicki, for her insight and enduring love and support. Second, I want to thank my students and former students with whom I have discussed these issues. I especially want to thank Professor Mark Bradbury of Appalachian State University, from whom I have learned much. Mark was able to read several chapters and offer insightful and helpful comments. I have benefited also from conversations with colleagues at the University of Georgia including Gene Brewer, George Krause, Tom Lauth, Jerry Legge, Hal Rainey, and Andy Whitford. Several of these friends took time from their busy schedules to read portions of the manuscript and offer valuable suggestions. Additional academic colleagues I am indebted to include Don Kettl, Lloyd Nigro, Steve Ott, Glenn Rainey, Bert Rockman, Jessica Sowa, and Frank Thompson. Others who have been directly involved with the issues covered in this work and have been extraordinarily helpful include Tristin Leavitt, Ron Sanders, James Sherk, and Julie Wilson. I owe a special thanks to Ron and James, who read portions of the book and tried their best to ensure that my story is accurate and honest. I hope I have met their expectations.

I also wish to thank all of the reporters and scholars whose work I have cited. They have added immeasurably to my understanding. In addition, this book is based in part on a journal article I published earlier; see, Kellough, J. Edward. (2023). "The Fragility of Merit: Erosion of the Foundation of Public Service Under Trump." *Review of Public Personnel Administration*, 0(0). https://doi.org/ 10.1177/0734371X231214973. Thanks also to Simon, my four-legged furry canine friend. He sat patiently by my desk for hours as I worked to complete this manuscript.

Finally, I am especially indebted to the late Paul P. Van Riper, whose classic *History of the United States Civil Service* has inspired me for years. Paul was a friend and mentor to me as my career was beginning and his was coming to a close. This book is, with respect and humility, dedicated to him.

J. Edward Kellough

June 11, 2024

Note

1 There are, of course, exceptions to this norm. A President may establish programs under standing authority by Executive Order. Presidents used Executive Orders as early as the 1940s to establish organizations to combat racial discrimination in federal employment. President Franklin D. Roosevelt's creation of the Fair Employment Practices Committee in 1941 is an example. Still, almost all federal agencies rely on legislative authorization and appropriations.

1

THE EVOLUTION OF THE U.S. PUBLIC SERVICE AND THE CONCEPT OF MERIT

The effectiveness of government in the United States (as in other countries) is dependent upon the presence of a competent and professionally oriented public workforce. The work of the U.S. government, whether it involves devising strategies to protect American interests internationally, safeguarding the American economy, developing programs to balance the national interest in environmental protection with the interests of private businesses, formulating policies to protect Americans from an unprecedented viral pandemic, or addressing a broad range of other public policy concerns, requires the application of expertise by dedicated men and women laboring in our governmental institutions. Politically neutral competence is a necessary foundation for the public service – needed today more than ever as the complexity of issues the government addresses continues to expand. However, reforms implemented during the administration of President Trump that were intended to strengthen presidential control were oriented toward establishing a more politicized federal civil service that would be more directly responsive to presidential policy priorities. While the operation and structure of the public workforce is not a matter that is foremost on the minds of most ordinary Americans, the consequences of various proposed civil service reforms for the nature and effectiveness of government are substantial. The traditional foundation of merit in federal employment, which at its most fundamental level requires that civil servants get their jobs based on demonstrated ability to perform those jobs rather than on political affiliation or loyalty, was placed at risk during the Trump years.

DOI: 10.4324/9781032656380-1

To better understand these developments and the nature of the U.S. federal civil service, it is helpful to view them through a historical lens and to consider briefly how the system evolved and developed over time.[1] When our constitutional structure for government was initially placed into operation under President George Washington on April 30, 1789, the responsibility for setting up an operational executive branch fell mainly to the new President, although the Congress exercised authority to establish the executive departments of government, specify their functions, and fund them by virtue of its legislative power granted in Article I of the Constitution. This distribution of authority is a reflection of the fact that the U.S. Constitution created a complex structure in which the power to govern is dispersed among three distinct institutions (or branches) of government with shared responsibilities. It is a system of separate yet overlapping authority that remains the footing for American government today. The U.S. Congress, for example, has primary responsibility for making laws through the legislative process, but the President can veto legislation and can issue executive orders directing action within the executive branch consistent with existing law. The judiciary has the responsibility for interpreting the law when it is challenged and determining its consistency with the Constitution, but the President nominates Supreme Court and lower-court judges for appointment, and the Senate must approve those nominees. The President, as head of the executive branch, must "take care that the laws be faithfully executed" (Article II, Section 3, U.S. Constitution), but Congress must authorize programs and appropriate money for their implementation, the Senate must confirm nominees for higher-level positions in federal departments and agencies, and the courts may review cases challenging the statutory or constitutional legitimacy of executive or Congressional action.

The Earliest Appointments

As President Washington set about the task of making initial presidential appointments to the departments established by Congress in 1789, he stressed "character, competence, and loyalty to the Constitution," but as Paul P. Van Riper points out, he also "paid deference to a desirable geographical distribution of appointments as well as to the opinions of senators, congressmen, and governors" in the states since most employees resided and worked outside of the federal capital (Van Riper, 1958, p. 18). In addition, Washington gave some preference to officers who had served under him during the Revolutionary War. In a letter dated November 30, 1789, Washington explained his approach to filling positions in the new government by stating, "In every nomination to office I have endeavored, as far as my own knowledge extended, or information could be obtained, to make *fitness of character* my primary object" (cited in White, 1956, p. 258) (emphasis added).[2] According to Leonard D. White, Washington also "set out to win esteem for the new government by appointing prominent citizens to office" (White, 1956, p. 317). Those appointed were typically men who were well-educated and relatively prosperous. As Frederick C. Mosher noted in his influential book *Democracy and the Public Service*, Washington established a "Government by Gentlemen" by placing men of the social and economic elite into positions in the federal service (Mosher, 1982, Chapter 3, pp. 58–64).

By the end of Washington's first term, a rudimentary system of two political parties had formed in Congress, with one group, the Federalists, coalescing around George Washington, John Adams, and Alexander Hamilton. The other faction, organized around Thomas Jefferson and James Madison, was known initially as the Republicans and later as the Democratic-Republicans. The groups differed over numerous issues, with the Federalists favoring a strong national government and the Democratic-Republicans preferring that the bulk of political authority rest at the state level where agrarian interests would be protected. This division had consequences for the civil service when, following his election as President in 1800 and his inauguration in 1801, Jefferson, who inherited a workforce of Federalists appointed by George Washington and John Adams, began dismissing those employees and replacing them with members of his party. Jefferson's goal was to seek a roughly equal distribution of adherents to each party within the public service, and this effort on his part was the first example of significant presidential use of the removal power established by Congress in 1789 (Van Riper, 1958, p. 22). Jefferson's actions underscored party affiliation or political patronage as a legitimate consideration in federal employee appointments. Otherwise, however, Jefferson maintained the criteria for appointment first specified by Washington. Reliance on members of the more elite segments of society continued. Subsequent Democratic-Republican presidents, James Madison and James Monroe, maintained this general approach, as did John Quincy Adams, whose party consisted of a conservative group that had split from the Democratic-Republicans, and which would eventually become known as the National Republicans.

In 1820, a growing Congressional interest in promoting political patronage as a basis for federal employment was demonstrated through passage of the Four Years Law, also known as the Tenure of Office Act of 1820. The law required that the term of office for a large number of specified positions in the executive branch be limited to four years, thus making those positions available for new patronage appointments where selection for employment would be based on political party affiliation. President Monroe signed the law but reportedly said he regretted doing so (Van Riper, 1958, p. 25).

John Quincy Adams competed for the Presidency in 1824 against Andrew Jackson of Tennessee and two other candidates.[3] While Jackson received a plurality of votes in the Electoral College, no candidate received a majority, and the U.S. House of Representatives decided the contest as required by the Constitution. Adams was chosen, and his success was partly attributed to the fact that Henry Clay, who had influence in the House and was staunchly opposed to Andrew Jackson, cast his support for Adams (Van Riper, 1958, p. 26). Later, the National Republicans (Adams' party), who continued to oppose Jackson, dissolved into the Whig Party.

The Triumph of Patronage

By 1828, many states had eased requirements for voting, extending the franchise to numerous white men who had been prevented from voting earlier by requirements mandating property ownership. Many of these new voters were aligned with Andrew Jackson. The presidential election of 1828 featured a rematch between Jackson and John Quincy Adams and was bitterly contested. Jackson prevailed by a comfortable margin, nevertheless, and his inauguration signaled a break with the past in several important ways, including the operation of the civil service. However, the reasons for that shift have much to do with Jackson's background and the political circumstances of his time.

Jackson was raised from humble origins. His mother and father immigrated to America from Ireland with his two older brothers in 1765. The family settled in a region known as Waxhaw in the Catawba River valley on the border between North and South Carolina. His father, who was injured in an accident while clearing land and working to establish a family homestead, died unexpectedly shortly before Jackson was born in 1767. His mother became dependent on a sister and her husband, who lived in the immediate area (Brands, 2005, pp. 15–16). As a result, "Jackson grew up an outsider, living on the margins and at the mercy of others" (Meacham, 2008, p. 8). When he was an adolescent, Jackson witnessed atrocities committed by the British near his home during America's war for independence. His oldest brother died at age 16 of heat exhaustion while fighting the British near Charleston. Later, the British imprisoned Jackson and his remaining brother, and both contracted smallpox. Their mother was able to secure their release, and although Jackson survived, his brother succumbed to the illness. Later, in the fall of 1781, his mother died of cholera while tending to her sister's sons, who were also held by the British (Brands, 2005, p. 30). At that point, Jackson had lost all of his immediate family as a result of the conflict with the British.

Shortly after the war, in 1785, Jackson, who had little formal education, apprenticed to an attorney to study law. Subsequently, at the age of 20, he was examined in the law by a two-judge panel and found competent to "plead and practice as an attorney" (Brands, 2005, p. 16). The following year, he relocated from the Carolinas to Nashville, Tennessee, where he began to build a new life and a career as a lawyer. In 1796, he was selected as a delegate to the Tennessee Constitutional Convention. Jackson was later elected to the U.S. House of Representatives and the U.S. Senate, although he resigned after serving in the Senate for only six months. He later served as a Superior Court Judge, was a Major General in the Tennessee state militia, and was a successful planter on an estate outside of Nashville known as "The Hermitage." During the War of 1812 against the British, Jackson was appointed Brigadier General in the U.S. Army. He delivered a crushing defeat to the British in the Battle of New Orleans on January 8, 1814, which made him a national hero (see Brands, 2005).

Jackson saw himself as a representative of the "common man" (Mosher, 1982, pp. 64–65; Van Riper, 1958, pp. 32–37). He identified closely with ordinary men and the soldiers who served under him, and they, in turn, admired his toughness and his dedication to them. As the biographer H. W. Brands states, Jackson was physically thin, but soldiers "saw in him a toughness, a resilience on which they could rely." He was compared to a hickory branch: "thin but impossible to break." Soon, he was known among his men by the affectionate moniker "Old Hickory" (Brands, 2005, p. 186).

Andrew Jackson's early life, his time at war, and his struggle to establish himself on the frontier in Tennessee all worked to inculcate a distaste for elite values and men of political privilege. After he was elected President, Jackson led a political faction known as the Democrats. This party supported agrarian interests and the preferences of states, especially those of states where slavery was practiced. Jackson inherited a civil service filled with individuals ideologically aligned with the beliefs of the Democratic-Republicans, National Republicans, and the followers of John Quincy Adams. There were no Democrats to be found, and Jackson viewed his election as a mandate for change (Van Riper, 1958, p. 31). He argued that democracy is better served by forcing turnover in the federal offices in order to install his supporters and party members. He saw this shift as a necessary reform, and he articulated an argument for it and the use of political patronage as a basis for appointment in the public service in an address to Congress on December 8, 1829, in which he famously stated:

> There are, perhaps, few men who can for any great length of time enjoy office and power without being more or less under the influence of feelings unfavorable to the faithful discharge of their public duties.
>
> *Van Riper (1958, p. 36)*

He continued by arguing,

> The duties of all public offices are, or at least admit of being made, so plain and simple that men of intelligence may readily qualify for their performance; and I cannot but believe that more is lost by the long continuance of men in office than is generally to be gained from their experience.
>
> *Van Riper (1958, p. 36)*

With this defense of political patronage articulated, Jackson set out to reshape the federal civil service by removing current officials and replacing them with his supporters. However, the best estimates suggest that he replaced less than 20 percent of the federal workforce (Eriksson, 1927). This application of the President's removal power was similar to what had occurred earlier under Jefferson. Nevertheless, Jackson had effectively defended the principle that the political victor was due the spoils of political conflict. Consistent with this argument, the subsequent rotation of party control of the White House gave rise to the federal patronage/spoils system in which removal and replacement of civil servants based on party affiliation became the dominant approach to filling government positions from the 1840s through the remainder of most of the nineteenth century. Political patronage was triumphant.

Table 1.1 lists U.S. Presidents of the eighteenth and nineteenth centuries, their years in office, and their party affiliations. As can be seen, there was regular rotation in office between the Democrats and their opposition, the Whig Party, during the 1840s and 1850s. Each time control of the Presidency changed, the newly elected President would remove appointees from the previous administration to replace them with supporters of their party. Presidents Harrison and Tyler (members of the Whig Party), for example, removed Democrats appointed

TABLE 1.1 U.S. Presidents through the Nineteenth Century

President	Years in Office	Party Affiliation
George Washington	1789–1797	Federalist
John Adams	1797–1801	Federalist
Thomas Jefferson	1801–1809	Democratic-Republican
James Madison	1809–1817	Democratic-Republican
James Monroe	1817–1825	Democratic-Republican
John Quincy Adams	1825–1829	National Republican
Andrew Jackson	1829–1837	Democrat
Martin Van Buren	1837–1841	Democrat
William Henry Harrison	1841	Whig
John Tyler	1841–1845	Whig
James K. Polk	1845–1849	Democrat
Zachary Taylor	1849–1850	Whig
Millard Fillmore	1850–1853	Whig
Franklin Pierce	1853–1857	Democrat
James Buchanan	1857–1861	Democrat
Abraham Lincoln	1861–1865	Republican
Andrew Johnson	1865–1869	National Union/Democrat
Ulysses S. Grant	1869–1877	Republican
Rutherford B. Hayes	1877–1881	Republican
James A. Garfield	1881	Republican
Chester A. Arthur	1881–1885	Republican
Grover Cleveland	1885–1889	Democrat
Benjamin Harrison	1889–1893	Republican
Grover Cleveland	1893–1897	Democrat
William McKinley	1897–1901	Republican

by Jackson and Van Buren. Harrison initiated the turnover, but his death after only one month in office meant that the task of completing the transition fell to Tyler. The Democrat, James K. Polk, followed Tyler into office, and he retaliated by removing Whig party appointees. The Whigs regained the Presidency with the election in 1848 of Zachary Taylor, who began the process of once more sweeping out Democratic appointees. Millard Fillmore, a Whig party affiliate who succeeded to the Presidency after Taylor died, continued the removal of Democrats. However, the Democrats returned to power in 1853, and Franklin Pierce retaliated against the Whigs. During this period, the offices changed every four years. There are no definitive data to tell us how extensive the forced turnover was, but it certainly reached all presidential offices and likely many layers below that level, given the President's influence and reach into the federal workforce. An administrative core of "comptrollers, auditors, and chief clerks" was maintained, nevertheless, to provide some "continuity and competence" in government (Van Riper, 1958, p. 51).

President Buchanan (a Democrat) took office in 1857, following fellow Democrat Franklin Pierce. Buchanan won the presidential nomination at the Democratic National Convention in 1856 in a struggle against Pierce. After his inauguration, Buchanan endorsed the principle of rotation in office every four years for individuals serving in the civil service and proceeded to remove President Pierce's appointees to replace them with his supporters. Pierce and Buchanan both worked to appease factions within the Democratic Party who opposed each other on the issue of slavery. Buchanan especially was sympathetic to politicians from slave-holding states and was opposed to agitation by abolitionists working to end slavery. Ultimately, the issue divided not only the Democratic Party but also the Nation itself.

During this time, a new political party, known as the Republicans, emerged in 1854. It was comprised of politicians opposed to the expansion of slavery into new states and western territories. Gradually, this party gained strength, especially from among former members of the Whig party, and in 1860, the Republican candidate for President, Abraham Lincoln, was elected. Following Lincoln's election, southern slave-holding states seceded from the Union, federal forces at Fort Sumpter, South Carolina, were attacked, and the country was plunged into civil war.

Given the unprecedented circumstances confronting Lincoln when he assumed the Presidency, political values and party affiliation were more critical than ever before when considering appointments to government positions. Support for the President and the Union were essential qualifications for office, and Lincoln set out to implement "the most complete sweep of the offices thus far" (Van Riper, 1958, p. 43). As Van Riper later notes, "From 1861 to 1865 the policy of [President] Washington, selection according to relative capacity and fitness, was almost entirely forgotten" (Van Riper, 1958, p. 43). Indeed, Van Riper suggests:

Lincoln appears to have used – or permitted the use of – the appointing powers at his command as deliberately as they could have been used for practical, and usually partisan, political purposes. The only thread of consistency in the executive appointing policy during the years from 1861 to 1865 seems to have been the practical one of preservation of the Union via preservation of the Republican party.

Van Riper (1958, p. 43)

For 20 years after Lincoln, the Republican party retained control of the Presidency, with the exception of the tenure of Andrew Johnson, a Democrat and National Union Party member, who served from 1865 to 1869 following Lincoln's assassination. During this time, political patronage was the expected basis for appointment to civil service positions. Office seekers lobbied personally at the White House for positions and enlisted the support of members of the House of Representatives and Senators from their home states. Partisan politics and public administration became tightly intertwined. Building from a foundation laid by Andrew Jackson, partisanship by civil servants was now expected and required. Civil servants were also obligated to make financial contributions, known as "political assessments," to the party organization that facilitated their employment (Van Riper, 1958, p. 46). The President sat atop this system, and patronage/spoils enhanced his political control of the government.

While the spoils system did not necessarily mean that competence and integrity were absent from the civil service ranks, those values were not preeminent, and there were problems, including corruption. Employment opportunities in government were traded for votes, promotions in the civil service were sold, employees in the customs houses and postal inspectors accepted bribes, unearned salaries were paid, and fraudulent purchases were made (White, 1958, pp. 272–275 and 366). The system of public employment was one in which competence and expertise were often subordinate to political allegiance or loyalty. In some instances, corruption reached high levels in the federal government, as in the infamous Crédit Mobilier of America scandal involving the Union Pacific Railroad Company, construction of the first transcontinental railroad, and the payment of bribes to members of Congress. In the scheme, which was exposed in 1872, executives of the Union Pacific Railroad created a fraudulent enterprise, Crédit Mobilier of America, to manage construction of the railroad. Crédit Mobilier overcharged the federal government by nearly double the actual cost of construction. The Union Pacific's executives pocketed the excess and used some of it to buy support from influential members of Congress.[4]

Following the Civil War, the country expanded rapidly geographically with the development of new territories and the admission of new states into the Union. Extensive steel and oil industries emerged, urbanization grew at an unprecedented pace, and new technologies, including those associated with the use of electricity, were developed. As the complexity of government's tasks increased in response to this growth, concern over inadequate abilities and expertise of public servants intensified. Rather than simple political loyalty, the need for government officials with skill and experience became increasingly apparent.

The Emergence of Merit

President Grant established a fledgling Civil Service Commission following passage by Congress in 1871 of a law that authorized the President to "prescribe such rules and regulations for the admission of persons into the civil service of the United States as will best promote the efficiency thereof" (quoted in Van Riper, 1958, p. 68). The Grant Commission established a preliminary set of civil service rules and instituted competitive examinations to measure skills necessary for the performance of selected jobs in Washington and in the customs house and post offices in the City of New York, which had been centers of corruption. Nevertheless, the desire for patronage led Congress to cut off funding for the Commission in 1873, and by 1875, the organization ceased to exist.

In subsequent years, President Hayes pushed Congress for civil service reform legislation but found little support from Republican Representatives and Senators for efforts that would diminish their influence over patronage. The extent of the reach of patronage was detailed by President Grant's first collector of customs in Baltimore, John L. Thomas, who stated in Congressional testimony that when he came to office in 1869, it was his responsibility to remove the Democrats that had been appointed previously by President Andrew Johnson. When asked if he removed all Democrats, he replied: "I believe I did" (quoted in White, 1958, p. 290). In a follow-up question, he was asked if many Democrats had been appointed since his tenure began. To this inquiry, he responded: "None that I know of. I did not appoint any" (White, 1958, p. 290). The patronage system was so deeply embedded in American politics at this point that substantial effort would be required to overturn it. As Leonard White explains:

> The forces that had to be overcome by the civil service reformers were enormous. The whole country was habituated to patronage from the experience of two generations. To a young man becoming aware of public affairs after the Civil War, patronage must have seemed the natural order for a republic.
>
> *White (1958, p. 291)*

One preliminary step that President Hayes took in favor of reform was to dispatch Dorman B. Eaton, a prominent advocate for civil service reform and the last head of Grant's Civil Service Commission, to report on the operation of the British civil service system and reforms that the British had implemented to ensure competence and expertise within the service (White, 1958, p. 288, note 35). Eaton's report was published in 1880. In addition, at the Republican Party nominating convention in 1880, the party endorsed reform despite substantial opposition. That action prompted a delegate from Texas, Mr. Flanagan, to exclaim, "What are we here for, if not to get the offices?" (White, 1958, p. 288). As a reaction or response to these kinds of attitudes, lobbying groups organized to direct attention to the excesses of spoils and to push for civil service reform across all levels of government.

In March of 1881, James A. Garfield was inaugurated as President of the United States. He had been a General in the Union Army during the Civil War and was a moderate advocate for reform of the civil service. Tragically, on July 2, 1881, Garfield was shot in the back and the right arm as he prepared to board a train for a trip to New Jersey. The assassin, Charles Guiteau, was a deranged ne'er-do-well who had lobbied the Garfield administration for an appointment as an American consul in Paris, France, even though he had no qualifications for such a position (Millard, 2011). After he fired his weapon, Guiteau was immediately apprehended, at which point he reportedly exclaimed, "I am a Stalwart of Stalwarts," and "Arthur is President now" (Bellamy, 2016). The Stalwarts, to which he pledged his allegiance, were a faction within the Republican party that supported the patronage/spoils system and had remained loyal to former President Grant. The reference to "Arthur," of course, is to Chester Arthur, a Stalwart and the former New York Collector of Customs and notorious spoilsman who had been removed from the New York Customs House by President Hayes for failing to follow a presidential order to refrain from collecting political assessments. Arthur was Garfield's Vice President, placed on the ballot in 1880 to balance the ticket and secure the support of New York Stalwarts. Garfield suffered with his wounds for more than two and a half months before dying on the evening of September 18, 1881. The assassination galvanized the Nation, and calls rose with increased intensity for reform of the partonage/spoils system. A National Civil Service Reform League was established in August of 1881 to push a reform agenda as a moral issue, partly as a reaction to what had happened to President Garfield.

Reform was eventually achieved, although it took time to come, and the motives for it were embedded deeply within the politics of the era. Because the Republican party had benefited from the patronage/spoils system for nearly 20 years, many within the party (the Stalwarts) were not eager to lose the advantages accompanying their control of patronage. The Democrats, on the other hand, enjoyed no benefits of the federal patronage system. Indeed, Democrats were among the strongest advocates for reform, and a Democratic Senator from Ohio, George H. Pendleton, introduced legislation calling for civil service reform as early as 1880, but the Republicans in control of the House of Representatives and the Senate were uninterested in the bill.

The Republican position on reform changed dramatically, however, following the mid-term election of 1882. Republican opposition to civil service reform became an issue in the election. Republicans were portrayed as supporters of the corruption and political abuse associated with the spoils system. When the votes were tallied, the Republican party was handed a significant defeat. They lost control of the House of Representatives to the Democrats. There was fear that the upcoming presidential election of 1884 would produce a Democratic president who would then sweep out all Republican officeholders (Van Riper, 1958, p. 94). In the face of these new political circumstances, the Republicans who remained in the House and Senate changed their view on civil service reform. They saw no wisdom in continuing to yield the moral high ground to the Democrats on the reform issue, and any legislation that would help protect Republican officeholders from removal if a Democrat was elected President in 1884 was undoubtedly attractive (Van Riper, 1958, p. 98). Mr. Pendleton revised his bill with the assistance of Dorman B. Eaton, and it was taken up and passed by both houses of Congress in December of 1882. In an act ripe with political irony, President Arthur, the notorious spoilsman, signed the bill into law on January 16, 1883.

The Pendleton Act of 1883 (22 Stat. 403, Chapter 27) established what has become known as a "merit system" in response to the corruption associated with the patronage/spoils system that relied on political loyalty as the primary criterion for selecting government workers. The term "merit" in this context indicates that public employees obtain their jobs based on demonstrated competence and are shielded from partisan political abuse. As outlined by Van Riper (1958), the merit system rests on three core principles:

1 *Selection of employees on the basis of the results of open and competitive examinations* designed to measure knowledge, skills, and abilities needed for job performance. The Act states: "Such examinations shall be practical in their character, and so far as may be shall relate to those matters which will fairly test the relative capacity and fitness of the persons examined to

discharge the duties of the service into which they seek to be appointed" (Pendleton Act, Section 2, 22 Stat. 403–404, Chapter 27).

2 *Political neutrality on the part of employees*: Section 2 of the Act contains the following language: "no person in the public service is … under any obligations to contribute to any political fund, or to render any political service, and that he will not be removed or otherwise prejudiced for refusing to do so," and "that no person in said service has any right to use his official authority or influence to coerce the political action of any person or body" (Pendleton Act, Section 2, 22 Stat. 404, Chapter 27).

3 *Relative security of tenure*, meaning that employees may not be discharged "for giving or withholding or neglecting to make any contribution of money or other valuable thing for any political purpose" (Pendleton Act, Section 13, 22 Stat. 407, Chapter 27). This is an important constraint on political removal, but otherwise the President's removal power was left intact. However, because employees covered by the Pendleton Act were selected only on the basis of open and competitive examinations, the incentive for political removal was diminished.

The merit system aimed to ensure politically neutral competence within the federal workforce. In short, the system was intended to limit the reach of partisanship into public management and to ensure the existence of a professionally competent public service.[5] Initially, the Pendleton Act covered only approximately ten percent of the federal civil service, but the law allowed presidents to expand (or retract) coverage. Republican fears that a Democrat could be elected in 1884 turned out to be well-founded. Grover Cleveland was elected that year, becoming the first Democratic President since the Civil War had ended. Before leaving office, the Republican Chester Arthur expanded coverage of the Pendleton Act to protect additional Republican employees. In subsequent years, as the parties rotated in control of the White House (see Table 1.1), the law's coverage was expanded further. Within 60 to 70 years, the merit system grew from covering only approximately 10 percent of the federal workforce to covering as much as 80 percent.

The Institutionalization of Merit

It is noteworthy that the Pendleton Act acknowledges presidential authority over personnel matters by *authorizing* the President to establish a merit system and a Civil Service Commission to implement that system but not *requiring* it. The Act includes language that the Civil Service Commission, if established, was to "aid the President, as he may request" in preparing rules for the federal service. It indicates that the Commission shall, "subject to the rules that may be made by the President," make regulations. In addition, the classification of positions under the law was to be made "on the direction of the President." Van Riper (1958, p. 105) argues that the Pendleton Act was written as "*permissive* rather than mandatory" (emphasis in original) to avoid questions about the statute's constitutionality since the Constitution vests appointment authority primarily in the hands of the President.

The Pendleton Act and the U.S federal merit system it established have been in place now for over140 years, and because it has covered the vast majority of the federal workforce for decades, and similar systems are implemented in state and local governments, the basic features and fundamental principles associated with merit are often accepted today as the "given" basis for public employment.[6] In short, a professional civil service resting on merit principles is seen as an established governmental institution. This idea does not mean, of course, that reforms calling for "flexibility" in public personnel management have not occurred. Merit rules are often viewed as placing excessive constraints on managers that produce an overly bureaucratic and rigid structure. Indeed, in some jurisdictions, dramatic reforms have been implemented, including the broad decentralization of authority for public human resources management policy away from central personnel management organizations down to line departments and agencies. In addition, some states have moved large segments of their public workforce to an at-will employment basis, eroding the concept of relative security of tenure for public employees (see Kellough and Nigro, 2006; Kim and Kellough, 2014; Nigro and Kellough, 2000). In an at-will system, employees can be fired "at will" for any reason, provided it is not an illegal reason or a reason that violates a collective bargaining contract. These measures, described as efforts to enhance managerial flexibility, are also often tied to efforts to enhance political control.

The merit system erected by the Pendleton Act does constrain political direction of the public workforce. That is, in large part, its purpose. The system was intended to curtail patronage by requiring that appointments be made based on demonstrated competence and by restricting political removal. However, the concept of merit is not the only feature of modern government that restricts political control. The issues that the government tackles today are often extraordinarily complex. The government formulates regulations to ensure the safety of food and drugs, protect the environment, regulate interstate commerce, manage the money supply, ensure the safety of consumer products, and manage threats to public health, to name only a few areas of concern.

More specifically, consider the work of the Nuclear Regulatory Commission charged with ensuring the safety of nuclear reactors or the tasks assigned to the Commodity Futures Trading Commission associated with protecting participants in the commodities and futures markets from manipulation and fraud. Also, consider the aeronautics and aerospace research carried out by the National Aeronautics and Space Administration (NASA). All of these tasks and organizations, and numerous others, require highly educated and technically competent employees.

The levels of specialized expertise necessary to carry out these functions mean that members of Congress and presidents are often at a disadvantage in evaluating and managing the actions taken by public servants. Politicians are rarely in a position to match the specialized expertise of the federal workforce. Congress, for example, through majority votes in each house and typically with presidential support, will establish government organizations and authorize programs, but the legislation passed cannot speak to every unforeseeable circumstance that may arise. Authority is always delegated to the agency or bureau to apply their expertise and use a measure of administrative discretion to implement programs and policies. Neither the Congress nor the President has the capacity to direct all administrative details.

Who, for example, would argue that a political officeholder with no knowledge of weather forecasts should predict the path of a hurricane? President Trump famously got into a dispute with the National Weather Service and the National Oceanic and Atmospheric Administration when he stated in late August of 2019 that Hurricane Dorian would possibly hit the state of Alabama. When evidence emerged that the National Weather Service forecast had not projected the storm would hit Alabama, the President insisted that he was correct and displayed what appeared to be an official forecast map on which the storm's expected path was altered with a sharpie to include an area of Alabama. As Don Kettl reminds us in his treatise on administrative expertise, "There was substantial political pressure on the National Oceanic and Atmospheric Administration, of which the Weather Service was a part, to change its forecast to match the president's pronouncement, and two top political appointees issued a statement that seemed to support Trump" (Kettl, 2023, p. 55). As a consequence, the scientific integrity of the National Oceanic and Atmospheric Administration was damaged (see Kettl, 2023, p. 55 and Freedman and Samenow, 2020).

As this outrageous story illustrates, we must have a public service selected on the basis of documented expertise. This approach is necessary given the complex nature of public problems *and* the incapacity of political actors to guide the specifics of program management knowledgeably. Because bureaucrats are experts and politicians are not, it is difficult for politicians to control the details of what bureaucrats do. Bureaucratic discretion over precise elements of policy implementation is, therefore, a fact of life in today's government (Rourke, 1984). This reality, combined with the need for a personnel system that stresses the selection of employees with demonstrated competence, makes political oversight difficult.

But oversight is possible. Politicians in elected positions retain numerous avenues of broad control of the bureaucracy, allowing them to set the direction for government. Congress authorizes programs and appropriates money for their operation. The President appoints the heads of departments and agencies and numerous other officials serving under the top-level officials. The President also heavily influences the budgetary process and can issue directives or executive orders requiring specific actions. In addition, the courts may rule on whether bureaucratic actions are consistent with statutes or the Constitution. These are all means of oversight and control of the bureaucracy.

Furthermore, research has shown that a public bureaucracy acting on the basis of professional expertise and working in cooperation with political authorities who exercise general oversight will produce the governing stability necessary for economic development and prosperity (Miller and Whitford, 2016). One problem, however, is that our confidence and faith in the security of fundamental principles of the merit system designed to ensure the presence of bureaucratic expertise may be greater than what is warranted. The foundation of merit is not as strong as we may wish to assume.

This book reviews the operation of the federal government's merit system and the constitutional basis for presidential power over the personnel function. It turns out that the system erected over the past 141 years is, in fact, quite fragile. That system presumes the presence of a President who understands and is committed to the concept of merit and has the political will to secure its preservation.[7]

Notes

1 Civil service systems in the states followed a similar path of development to that of the federal system, although state systems lagged behind the federal system, sometimes by several decades, in terms of their evolution.

2 This statement is in a letter to Joseph Jones of Virginia in which Washington explained in detail his reasons for selecting a candidate for a District Judgeship other than Mr. Jones. The text of this letter is located at: https://founders.archives.gov/documents/Washington/05-03-02-0082#GEWN-05-03-02-0082-sn.

3 The other candidates were William H. Crawford of Georgia and Henry Clay of Kentucky.

4 For a full examination of this matter, see Mitchell, Robert B. 2017. *Congress and the King of Frauds: Corruption and the Crédit Mobilier Scandal at the Dawn of the Gilded Age*. (Roseville, Minn.: Edinborough Press).

5 Research has demonstrated that the merit system can enhance employee attitudes and motivation, reduce turnover intentions, and improve the quality performance (e.g., Alexander and Ruderman, 1987; Brewer, Kellough, and Rainey, 2022; Rainey, 1997).

6 A review of popular public sector human resources management textbooks will confirm this perception. See, e.g., Battaglio, 2015; Berman, Bowman, West, and Van Wart, 2022; Cayer and Sabharwal, 2016; Llorens, Klingner, and Nalbandian, 2018; Riccucci, Naff, and Hamidullah, 2020; Nigro and Kellough 2014.

7 This point was made 140 years ago by the prominent civil service reform advocate George William Curtis in testimony before the Senate Committee on Civil Service and Retrenchment in 1882 during consideration of the Pendleton Act (see Van Riper, 1958, p. 108).

2

PERSONNEL IS POWER

Controlling Government by Controlling the Civil Service

Paul P. Van Riper titled the final chapter in his *History of the United States Civil Service*, "Personnel is Power – A Theory of Governmental Reform" (Van Riper, 1958, Chapter 17). In this conclusion to his sweeping review of the development and evolution of the federal civil service, Van Riper declared 66 years ago, "the many and acrimonious quarrels over public office during the course of American history only underline the fact that he who administers the law is often more important than the law itself" (p. 533). In effect, the power to appoint and direct public employees is the power to direct government action and public policy. It is no wonder that there continues to be debate over the operation and control of the civil service. The title of this chapter of the present book is borrowed in part from Van Riper's final chapter.

President Trump famously said in the summer of 2019, "I have an Article II, where I have the right to do whatever I want as President" (Brice-Saddler, 2019). While Trump's description of Presidential power was inflated and inaccurate, since a President may not "do whatever" he/she wants, there is, indeed, a school of thought known as the "unitary executive theory," which holds that the President has unparalleled authority over the entire executive branch (Crouch, Rozell and Sollenberger, 2020; Skowronek, Dearborn and King, 2021). In the most uncompromising versions of this theory, Congress may not limit the President's ability to direct executive departments and agencies (and their personnel) because the Constitution bestows that power

DOI: 10.4324/9781032656380-2

exclusively on the President. Proponents of this argument point to the Constitution's grant of "executive power" to the President found in Article II, Section 1, and the directive in Article II, Section 3 that the President "shall take care that the laws be faithfully executed." This view of presidential authority discounts the constitutional system of distinct but overlapping and shared powers of the three branches of government. It has provided a basis for the justification of a wide range of presidential actions by chief executives of both parties. However, it is especially the case that beginning in the 1980s political conservatives have embraced the unitary executive theory to justify expansive interpretations of presidential control of the federal civil service, which includes not only the power to appoint but also the power to remove public employees.

Specific provisions in the Constitution outline a complex system regarding the filling of positions within the executive branch. The Constitution of the United States provides only minimal guidance, but in doing so, distributes authority between the President and the Congress. Article II, Section 2 describes the President's appointment authority by stating:

> he shall nominate, and by and with the Advice and Consent of the Senate, shall appoint Ambassadors, other public Ministers and Consuls, Judges of the Supreme Court, and all other Officers of the United States, whose Appointments are not herein otherwise provided for, and which shall be established by Law....

However, the Constitution also specifies a role for Congress. Article II, Section 2 includes the following passage immediately after the grant of presidential appointment authority:

> but the Congress may by Law vest the Appointment of such inferior Officers, as they think proper, in the President alone, in the Courts of Law, or in the Heads of Departments.

Notably, the provision indicating that Congress may assign appointment authority for "inferior Officers ... in the President alone, in the Courts of Law, or in the Heads of Departments" created from the very beginning two broad categories of federal officials – those that are presidentially appointed with the advice and consent of the Senate and those who are in lessor positions and are appointed by the President or other officials without approval by the Senate. However, to describe the extent of presidential appointments in the early years of the Republic, Paul P. Van Riper estimated that the "offices of the presidential class," which were positions in the federal civil service "whose incumbents were appointed directly by the president" comprised approximately *ten percent* of the entire workforce from 1800 to 1810 (Van Riper, 1958, pp. 22 and 23, note 29). This "presidential" category included appointees who required Senate confirmation and those for whom Senate confirmation was not required. Van Riper continued by noting:

> In general, the most important offices are among those found in the presidential class. In the early eighteen hundreds, offices held by cabinet members, postmasters, collectors of customs and internal revenue, territorial and foreign officers, district attorneys, marshals, naval officers (civil), surveyors, and a few other types of personnel fell into this class.
>
> *Van Riper (1958, pp. 22, 23, note 29)*

The remaining ninety percent of the workforce was "appointed by other officers in the executive branch, as designated by Congress under the terms of the Constitution" (Van Riper, 1958, pp. 22, 23, note 29). However, one could expect that when the heads of departments made appointments, they would follow selection criteria established by the President, which is precisely what happened. According to the public administration historian Leonard D. White, "For top appointments they [the Presidents] were their own personnel officers; for intermediate appointments and many lesser ones they were consulted, and their preferences were directly controlling" (White, 1954, p. 74). Thus, presidential influence extended far beyond those the President appointed directly. Indeed, Presidents were at times consulted even regarding the appointment of "rank-and-file employees in the field offices" (White, 1954, p. 74).

Who Are "Officers of the United States?"

In the earliest days of our republic, all individuals who worked for the federal government were appointed under the provisions of Article II, Section 2 of the Constitution. In a comprehensive review of the meaning of these provisions, Jennifer L. Mascott argues persuasively that "In the Founding era, the term 'Officer' was commonly understood to encompass any individual who had ongoing responsibility for a governmental duty" (Mascott, 2018, p. 450). This understanding included those at the top of federal departments and agencies and those in lesser positions. Some officers were at a high level, and some were "inferior" officers, but all were officers of the government.

Nevertheless, in the modern era, controversy has developed over the precise meaning of the terms in the constitutional provisions governing appointments. Through a series of Supreme Court decisions, the Court has defined three categories of individuals who work for the federal government. First, according to the Supreme Court, individuals who hold an office established by law and who exercise "significant authority" are "Officers of the United States" within the meaning of Article II, Section 2 of the Constitution (*Buckley* v. *Valeo*, 424 U.S. 1 (1976) at 126). Second, persons who are supervised by an "Officer of the United States" and for whom Congress has determined a selection method are "Inferior Officers" under the Constitution (*Edmond* v. *United States*, 520 U.S. 651 (1997) at 663). Finally, there are "employees" who serve as "lesser functionaries subordinate to officers" (see *Buckley* v. *Valeo*, 424 U.S. 1, Footnote 162 and *United States* v. *Germaine*, 99 U.S. 508 (1879)).

The precise definition of "employees" is elusive, however. In addition, the distinction made by the Supreme Court suggests that "employees" may be appointed through processes other than those specified in Article II, Section 2 of the Constitution. But if that is the case, how are those appointments made? In short, in seeking to clarify matters, the Court introduced considerable ambiguity into the filling of positions in the federal service. If the Court views "employees" as individuals hired under our civil service laws, it is essential to note that, as we shall see, the existence and organization of the civil service system are matters of presidential prerogative.

The President's Removal Power

The Constitution is silent on the removal of federal officials except for provisions for impeachment of the "President, Vice President and all civil Officers of the United States" (Article II, Section 4). While the definition of which employees are counted as "civil officers" was unclear, it apparently did not refer to the bulk of the federal workforce, at least in the minds of many of the Framers of the Constitution. Indeed, Congress passed legislation in its first session in 1789 implying that the President had the power to remove all federal employees, including those appointed with Senate confirmation.[1]

The argument over removal power that gave rise to this legislation arose as Congress considered the establishment of the first federal departments: Foreign Affairs, War, and Treasury. The bills to establish these departments contained language implying that the President may remove executive branch officials, but whether the authority to do so was derived from the Constitution or was granted by Congress was unclear. In fact, it may be that the lack of clarity was necessary to secure passage in the Senate (Shugerman, 2020). Passage of the bill creating the Department of Foreign Affairs, for example, was by the thinnest of margins. The Senate vote was tied at 10 to 10, and the bill passed only with a tie-breaking vote by Vice President Adams (Shugerman, 2020). Because this was the first of the bills considered regarding the creation of executive departments, it is of primary importance, and subsequent bills establishing the Department of War and the Department of the Treasury contained language similar to that regarding the Foreign Affairs Department. The separate bills for the three departments were referred to collectively as the "legislative decision of 1789" or simply, the "decision of 1789." The full text of the legislation establishing the Department of Foreign Affairs (with the portion referring to presidential removal power in italics) reads as follows:

An ACT for establishing an Executive Department, to be denominated the Department of Foreign Affairs.

BE it enacted by the Senate and House of Representatives of the United States of America in Congress assembled, That there shall be an executive department, to be denominated the department of foreign affairs, and that there shall be a principal officer therein, to be called the Secretary for the department of foreign affairs, who shall perform and execute such duties as shall, from time to time, be enjoined on or entrusted to him by the President of the United States, agreeable to the Constitution, relative to correspondences, commissions or instructions, to or with public ministers or consuls, from the United States, or to negotiations with public ministers from foreign States or princes, or to memorials or other applications from foreign public ministers, or other foreigners, or to such other matters respecting foreign affairs, as the President of the United States shall assign to the said department: And furthermore, that the said principal officer shall conduct the business of the said department in such manner as the President of the United States shall, from time to time, order or instruct.

And be it further enacted, That there shall be, in the said department, an inferior officer, to be appointed by the said principal officer, and to be employed therein as he shall deem proper, and to be called the chief clerk in the department of foreign affairs, *and who whenever the said principal officer shall be removed from office by the President of the United States,* or in any other case of vacancy, shall, during such vacancy, have the charge and custody of all records, books and papers appertaining to the said department. And be it further enacted, That the said principal officer, and every other person to be appointed or employed in the said department, shall, before he enters on the execution of his office or employment, take an oath or affirmation, well and faithfully to execute the trust committed to him.

And be it further enacted, That the Secretary for the department of foreign affairs, to be appointed in consequence of this act, shall forthwith after his appointment, be entitled to have the custody and charge of all records, books and papers in the office of Secretary for the department of foreign affairs, heretofore established by the United States in Congress assembled.

United States Statutes at Large, Volume 1, 1st Congress, 1st Session

Clearly, this language suggests that the President may remove the highest-level officials. Whether that power requires Senate approval for the removal of an official appointed with Senate confirmation is unclear. The most that can be said is that the law does not say that Senate approval is required. This issue was central to the conflict between President Andrew Johnson, who succeeded Lincoln in office, and the Republican majority in Congress at that time. President Johnson, who was from the South, differed from the Republicans regarding policies associated with the integration of southern states back into the union and reconstruction. Johnson used his control of patronage to further his policy priorities, and in response, in 1867, Congress passed the Tenure of Office Act over Johnson's veto. The law required Senate approval for the President's removal of any official appointed with Senate confirmation. After Johnson attempted to remove Secretary of War Edwin Stanton without Senate approval, Republicans in the House of Representatives impeached the President, who ultimately survived a trial in the Senate by the thinnest of margins – one vote. The failure of the Senate to convict Johnson may be seen as an acknowledgment of unrestricted presidential removal power, albeit a very weak one (Van Riper, 1958, p. 67). The Tenure of Office Act was eventually repealed in 1887, an action that also implied congressional acceptance of presidential authority over removal grounded in the Decision of 1789, but the issue was far from definitively resolved.

In 1876, Congress passed a law providing that postmasters of the first, second, and third classes whom the President appointed with Senate confirmation could only be removed by the President if the Senate consented to the removal. These positions in the Postal Service were prime patronage targets. Decades later, President Woodrow Wilson removed a postmaster first class (Frank S. Myers) without seeking Senate approval. Myers challenged his dismissal in Court, and the case eventually went to the U.S. Supreme Court in *Myers* v. *United States* (272 U.S. 52 (1926)). The issue was whether the 1876 law imposed an unconstitutional constraint on the President's power to remove officials without Senate approval when they had earlier been appointed with that approval.

The case was decided in 1926. Former President William Howard Taft, then the Chief Justice of the United States Supreme Court, wrote for the majority that the President's removal authority was grounded in the Constitution and could not be limited by Congress (*Myers* v. *United States* (272 U.S. 52 (1926)). Under this interpretation, the President had an unconstrained power of dismissal that was deemed essential to his executive authority and to the constitutional requirement that he "shall take care that the laws be faithfully executed" (U.S. Constitution, Article 2, Section 3). In effect, the majority in *Myers* said that the Constitution empowers the President to remove any executive officer appointed by him, even if that appointment was made with the advice and consent of the Senate, and Congress may not limit this power. The decision in *Myers* indicated that the Tenure of Office Act of 1867, which required Senate approval for presidential removal of any officer previously appointed with Senate confirmation, was unconstitutional, as was the law from 1876 prohibiting presidential removal of postmasters of the first, second, and third classes appointed with the advice and consent of the Senate. This ruling was a landmark endorsement of presidential authority.

Nevertheless, in a significant move in 1935, the Supreme Court backed away from the *Myers* decision. This development occurred in the case known as *Humphrey's Executor vs. United States* (295 U.S. 602 (1935)). The facts of the case concerned Mr. William E. Humphrey, who had been appointed a Federal Trade Commission (FTC) commissioner by President Hoover and confirmed by the Senate in 1931. In 1933, President Roosevelt determined that Humphrey was insufficiently supportive of several of the President's New Deal initiatives. Roosevelt requested Humphrey's resignation, and after Humphrey refused, Roosevelt fired him. However, the legislation establishing the FTC allowed a president to remove a commissioner only for "inefficiency, neglect of duty, or malfeasance in office." The question before the Court was whether the FTC Act unconstitutionally interfered with the President's removal power. Humphrey died shortly after being dismissed, and his executor sued to recover Humphrey's lost salary, hence the reference to "Humphrey's Executor" in the case title.

A unanimous Supreme Court found that the FTC Act was constitutional and that Humphrey's dismissal on policy grounds violated the law.

The government's main argument relied heavily on the Court's decision in *Myers,* where, as we have seen, the Court upheld the President's right to remove officers from the executive branch of government. In *Humphrey's Executor*, however, the Court argued that the FTC was different because it performed quasi-legislative and judicial functions by issuing regulations and adjudicating disputes arising from the application of those regulations. Hence, the *Myers* precedent was distinguished from the situation in this case, and the Court in *Humphrey's Executor* articulated a significant limitation on the President's power of removal.

Nonetheless, this struggle to define presidential authority over the removal of executive employees was not over. Years later, in a significant case decided in 2010, the Supreme Court strengthened presidential removal power. This case was *Free Enterprise Fund* v. *Public Company Accounting Oversight Board* (561 U.S. 477 (2010)). The structure of the Public Company Accounting Oversight Board, which was created in 2002 as part of the Sarbanes–Oxley Act (116 Stat. 745), was at issue. The Act was passed in response to several widely publicized corporate and accounting scandals, including fraudulent accounting practices that led to the collapse of the Enron Corporation in the fall of 2001. Enron had utilized accounting procedures that concealed billions of dollars in debt from stockholders, and that led ultimately to what was, at the time, the largest corporate bankruptcy in U.S. history and the demise of the nationally known Arthur Anderson Accounting firm. Enron's shareholders lost tens of billions of dollars, and its employees lost billions more in retirement benefits.

The Public Company Accounting Oversight Board (the Board) was established to protect investors from fraudulent accounting practices such as those used at Enron by establishing and enforcing new auditing and financial regulations for publicly held corporations. All accounting firms that audit publicly held companies were required to register with the Board, pay an annual fee, and comply with the Board's regulations. The Board consisted of five members appointed by the Securities and Exchange Commission (SEC) who are removable by the SEC only for good cause. Members of the SEC, who are appointed by the President, are also removable only for just cause. Thus, there were two layers of constraint on the President's power to remove members of the Board.

The Free Enterprise Fund, a nonprofit association of accounting firms, brought suit against the Public Company Accounting Oversight Board after one of its member firms (Beckstead and Watts of Nevada) came under investigation by the Board. The Free Enterprise Fund argued that the organizational structure of the Board violated the Constitution because the dual layers of for-cause removal restrictions imposed an undue constraint on the President's executive power. Chief Justice John Roberts, writing for a 5–4 majority, found that members of the Board are "Officers of the United States" within the meaning of Article II of the Constitution since they "exercise significant authority pursuant to the laws of the United States" and that their "multilevel protection from removal is contrary to Article II's vesting of the executive power in the President. The President cannot 'take Care that the Laws be faithfully executed' if he cannot oversee the faithfulness of the officers who execute them" (561 U.S. 484). In effect, the Court reasoned that the President's authority includes the ability to control "officers" in the executive branch through removal or the threat of removal.

More recently, the Supreme Court again addressed the issue of the President's removal power in *Seila Law LLC* v. *the Consumer Financial Protection Bureau* (591 U.S. ____, 2020; 140 S. Ct. 2183). This case presented a challenge to the structure of the Consumer Financial Protection Bureau (CFPB), which provided that the agency be headed by a single Director who could be removed by the President only for cause defined in the statute as "inefficiency, neglect of duty, or malfeasance in office" (124 Stat. 1964).

The CFPB was established in 2010 as an independent agency charged with regulating the financial sector to protect the interests of consumers. The agency was created in Section 110 of the "Dodd – Frank Wall Street Reform and Consumer Protection Act," which was a legislative response to the financial crisis and "Great Recession" that began in 2008 (124 Stat. 1376). The CFPB was established as a bureau within the Federal Reserve System. The agency's mission is to write and enforce rules for financial institutions and to collect and investigate consumer complaints. Among other actions, the agency worked to end abusive debt collection practices and reformed the mortgage lending industry.

In 2017, the CFPB was investigating Seila Law LLC, a California law firm providing debt-related legal services to clients. During the investigation, the CFPB issued a "civil investigative demand," similar to a subpoena, to require the firm to provide information and documents related to its business practices so that the CFPB could determine if the firm had engaged in unlawful acts or practices in the advertising, marketing, or sale of debt relief services. Seila Law refused to comply, and the CFPB filed a petition in the U.S. District Court for the Central District of California to enforce compliance. Seila Law argued that submission to the CFPB was not necessary because the agency Director's exercise of authority to compel compliance while at the same time being insulated from presidential removal was a violation of the Constitution's separation of powers doctrine. In essence, since the CFPB was an independent agency exercising substantial executive power and headed by a Director whom the President could not remove except for specific cause, the law creating the CFPB imposed an unconstitutional constraint on the President's executive authority. The district court ruled in favor of the CFPB and ordered Seila Law to comply with the request for information and documents. Seila Law appealed the District Court's order to the Ninth Circuit Court of Appeals, but the Ninth Circuit agreed with the decision of the District Court. Seila Law then appealed to the U.S. Supreme Court.

The Supreme Court addressed two issues. The first question was whether the legislation establishing the CFPB as an independent agency headed by a single Director shielded from presidential removal (except for specific cause) constitutes an improper congressional constraint on the President's executive authority in violation of the separation of powers principle. The second question was whether the provision in the law limiting the President's removal power could be separated or severed from the remainder of the authorizing legislation.

In a 5 to 4 decision, the Court ruled in favor of Seila Law. The CFPB's leadership by a single Director, removable only for inefficiency, neglect, or malfeasance, did violate the Constitution because it established an unwarranted restriction on the power of the President. Writing for the conservative majority, Chief Justice John Roberts held that "the entire 'executive Power' belongs to the President alone" (*Seila Law*, Part III, A). Furthermore, the majority argued that lower-level officers within the executive branch "must remain accountable to the President, whose authority they wield" (*Seila Law*, Part III, A). Chief Justice Roberts concluded the majority opinion by arguing that "In our constitutional system, the executive power belongs to the President, and that power generally includes the ability to supervise and remove the agents who wield executive power in his stead" (591 U. S. ____ (2020), Slip Opinion, p 37). In reaching that conclusion, Roberts relied on the Court's earlier decisions in *Myers* and *Free Enterprise Fund*. Roberts reasoned that the ruling in *Humphrey's Executor*, which permitted a congressional constraint on the President's removal power, was not applicable because the FTC of 1935 was deemed to perform legislative and judicial functions rather than executive responsibilities.

Other efforts to limit presidential removal power, for instance, through Executive Orders from Presidents McKinley and Theodore Roosevelt requiring that dismissal be for cause only, are not impacted by the *Myers* and subsequent related decisions since those orders were undertaken at presidential discretion and can be revoked at presidential discretion.

However, the requirement that removals of employees be for just cause (i.e., for reasons that promote the efficiency of the civil service) was later incorporated explicitly into the Lloyd–LaFollette Act of 1912 (see Van Riper, 1958, pp. 144, 217, Executive Order 101, Executive Order 173, Lloyd–LaFollette Act 1912).[2] The Lloyd–LaFollette Act states in part, "no person in the *classified civil service* of the United States shall be removed therefrom except for such cause as will promote the efficiency of said service" (emphasis added). But importantly, as was explained in Chapter 1, the classified civil service is established under and includes individuals appointed ultimately at the direction of the President.

Still, there are interesting questions about the distinction between civil service "employees" and "Officers of the United States" (or Inferior Officers, for that matter) within the meaning of the Constitution. The Court noted in *Free Enterprise* that "many civil servants within independent agencies would not qualify as 'Officers of the United States'" (561 U.S. 506). The Court further stressed that "Nothing in our opinion, therefore, should be read to cast doubt on the use of what is colloquially known as the civil service system within independent agencies" (561 U.S. 507). As we have observed, the Court has defined "Officers of the United States" as officials who "exercise significant authority pursuant to the laws of the United States" (*Free Enterprise* (561 U.S. 484)). The Court has also stated that "inferior officers are officers whose work is directed and supervised at some level by other officers appointed by the President with the Senate's consent" (see the 1997 decision in *Edmond* v. *United States*, (520 U.S. 662–663) as cited in *Free Enterprise* (561 U.S. 510)). Issues central to democratic governance related to questions of political control and accountability for government action hinge directly on the relationship of the President to the federal civil service.

The President and the Civil Service

Republican politicians and conservatives, regardless of party, have long argued that the merit system provides federal employees excessive protections from removal.[3] According to this claim, terminating federal employees or otherwise holding them accountable is much too difficult. Political control of the government bureaucracy, which properly belongs to the President, is more complex than it should be (see, e.g., Devine, 2017). It is argued that conservative Presidents' policy agendas may be obstructed by employees charged with responsibility for developing and implementing regulations, making it difficult for conservatives to achieve policy objectives.

There is a well-organized constituency sympathetic to this view. This constituency includes business leaders as well as conservative legal scholars and intellectuals at policy institutes or research/advocacy organizations. They draw upon ideas central to the unitary executive theory to advocate for dramatic reform to make the federal workforce more responsive to political direction. They argue that the President has ample constitutional authority to control the civil service directly. The Heritage Foundation, for example, sponsored a panel discussion on the need for federal administrative reform consistent with the conservative agenda (including civil service reform) on August 15, 2017 (The Heritage Foundation, 2017). They also published two reports advocating for comprehensive reforms for the "bloated and lethargic" federal service (Muhlhausen, 2017a, p. 1, 2017b). From the perspective of scholars at the Heritage Foundation and similar organizations, the merit system should not operate to shield the civil service from political control to the extent that it does currently. Efforts by conservatives to weaken civil service rules and procedures are part of a long-term effort by economic and corporate interests to weaken government or weaken the ability of government to pursue policies contrary to their interests.

In large part, the dispute that conservatives have with the "administrative state" is grounded on opposition to the vast range of regulations issued by the government and its agencies. Regulations today cover an immense range of issues. There are, for example, occupational safety and health regulations covering manufacturing and other firms. There are also banking regulations, the regulation of meat, dairy, and other food products, the regulation of drugs and pharmaceuticals, regulations limiting air and water pollution, and countless other regulations that address nearly every aspect of life. These regulations always impose costs on the producers of goods and services, and those costs are not passed on entirely to consumers. Businesses generally oppose having to bear any of those costs.

As a consequence, there are well-defined and powerful groups who want to see regulations eliminated or reduced. The Republican party and conservatives generally have represented those constituencies and their interests for several decades. William Howell and Terry Moe made an insightful argument recently related to this issue when they observed in an essay for the Washington Post that:

For much of American history, government was skeletal and primitive. But by the late 1800s, as policymakers struggled to deal with the searing problems of modernity, progressive reformers sought to create a more effective

government and an expert, professionalized bureaucracy capable of convert-
ing problem-solving policies into action. This bureaucracy was significantly
expanded by the New Deal, the Great Society, and major regulatory programs of the 1970s, yielding a massive administrative state that by 1980 had
grown to maturity.

Howell and Moe (2021)

Howell and Moe continue by noting that:

except for the defense and national security agencies, the administrative state
embodies Democratic commitments and values: the protection of workers,
consumers and the environment, the regulation of business, aid to the poor
and more. When Democrats look out upon the administrative state, they see
allies performing vital government functions. When Republicans do so, they
see enemies intruding on the private sector and threatening individual liberties.

Howell and Moe (2021)

The recent focus by political conservatives and Republicans generally on
the unitary executive theory and expansive versions of that theory positing
that the President has control over everything within the executive branch
and that Congress may not constrain the President's power to direct the federal
bureaucracy and its personnel is simply the latest and most direct attack on
government policies that impose regulatory costs on industrial and business
interests they support and legislation that appropriates federal resources for
social programs to aid the underprivileged. The goal is to eliminate regulations, reduce taxes, and limit or curtail federal government expenditures to
assist people experiencing poverty. The conservative argument is that the
President should use available constitutional authority to direct government
personnel to push the federal bureaucracy in these preferred policy directions.
Control is to be achieved by reducing federal employee rights, constraining
the power of employee unions, and ultimately, through the threat of removal
(if not actual removal) of employees.

Recently, the conservative attack on regulation was fought on yet another
front. Conservatively oriented public interest law firms sought to overturn an
important legal precedent set in 1984 which established that the courts will give
deference to the expertise of government agencies who must interpret ambiguous
statutes when issuing regulations, provided that the interpretations by agencies
are reasonable. This principle, known as Chevron Deference, was established
in *Chevron U.S.A., Inc. v. National Resources Defense Council* (467 U.S. 837).

In the fall of 2023, the U.S. Supreme Court agreed to hear two cases that directly challenged the *Chevron* decision. These cases were *Loper Bright Industries* v. *Raimondo* (No. 22-452) and *Relentless Inc.* v. *Department of Commerce* (No. 22-1219). Arguments in *Loper Bright* and *Relentless* were heard by the Supreme Court on January 17, 2024. The petitioners were two fishing companies from New Jersey and Rhode Island who were challenging a decision that required them to pay the costs of having federal monitors on their boats to ensure that they comply with a law intended to prevent overfishing. This decision was made by the National Marine Fisheries Service, an agency within the U.S. Department of Commerce. The fishing companies found the costs were unreasonable, but the U.S. District Courts and Courts of Appeals hearing the cases, following the ruling in *Chevron*, deferred to the agency's expertise and ruled that the imposition of the cost on the fishing industry was based on a permissible interpretation of the agency's legislative mandate. When the Supreme Court agreed to hear these cases, it indicated that it would reconsider the appropriateness of judicial deference to administrative expertise required by the *Chevron* ruling. A reversal of the *Chevron* decision would mean that deference would no longer be given to agency expertise in the interpretation of ambiguous statutory requirements. Such a ruling would be congruent with the Supreme Court's reliance in recent years on what is known as the "Major Questions Doctrine," a judicial construction dating from the year 2000 that requires courts to assume that Congress does not delegate to executive branch regulatory agencies the authority to decide issues of major political or economic significance (see *FDA* v. *Brown & Williamson Tobacco Corp.* (529 U.S. 120, 2000) and *West Virginia* v. *Environmental Protection Agency* (597 U.S. ____, 2022).

On June 28, 2024, the U.S. Supreme Court announced its decision in the *Loper Bright* and *Relentless* cases. The principle of *Chevron* Deference was overturned. The majority, consisting of Chief Justice Roberts and Associate Justices Thomas, Alito, Gorsuch, Kavanaugh, and Barrett, found that the requirement that courts defer to the expertise of administrative agencies in disputes over agency actions was a violation of the Administrative Procedures Act of 1946 that required the courts to decide "all relevant questions of law" when reviewing agency actions (5 United States Code, Section 706). The majority argued further that it is the courts rather than executive agencies that have competence in resolving legislative ambiguities. Associate Justice Jackson took no part in the *Loper Bright* decision, but Associate Justices Kagan and Sotomayor dissented. In the *Relentless* case, all three of the liberal Associate Justices, Kagan, Sotomayor, and Jackson dissented. This outcome does not mean, however, that agencies will no longer rely on their expertise when making decisions in the implementation of ambiguous statutes. But the courts will no longer be required to defer to agency interpretations. Still, the courts are likely to recognize agency expertise when rendering their own decisions, and judicial interpretation will not necessarily always replace bureaucratic expertise. The courts are, however, likely to continue to rely on the Major Questions Doctrine as outlined by the Supreme Court, and that approach, combined with the *Loper Bright* and *Relentless* decisions, could curb agency discretion in the interpretation of ambiguous legislation – an outcome currently favored by conservatives. Ironically, the *Chevron* ruling was viewed originally as serving the conservative agenda because it upheld a conservative interpretation of law by the Environmental Protection Agency during the administration of President Ronald Reagan.

In the following pages, this book will review these issues in the context of efforts to reshape the federal civil service during the Trump Presidency. The Trump years were tumultuous for several reasons, but one reason certainly was the concerted effort the Administration and its Republican allies in Congress engaged in to fundamentally alter the structure and operation of the federal merit system. Five specific events are reviewed: (1) the disabling of the Merit Systems Protection Board (MSPB) – the administrative board that hears appeals from employees of adverse personnel actions, (2) the President's Executive Orders of May 25, 2018, designed to weaken federal employee unions and to make it easier to fire federal workers, (3) the effort from 2018 through 2020 to dismantle the U.S. Office of Personnel Management – the government's central human resources management agency – and place authority over personnel policy within the Office of Management and Budget in the Executive Office of the President, (4) the establishment late in 2020 of "Schedule F," a new employment category within the Excepted Service which was to receive large segments of the federal workforce housed previously in the Competitive Service, and (5) The Trump Administration's effort to reorient the Federal Labor Relations Authority to weaken the position of federal employee unions.

In the end, the fact remains: If you can control how employees are selected, assigned, and managed, and how they can be disciplined or dismissed, then you can control how they perform their duties and how policy is implemented. This truth lies at the heart of struggles over control of the civil service. In working to redirect personnel policy, the Trump Administration had an ally in the Republican-controlled Senate in 2017 and 2018. One of the most direct mechanisms of influence the Senate has over the public workforce is the confirmation process required for a large portion of presidential appointees. That process is, of course, highly politicized and, as we shall see, was wholly dysfunctional in the case of President Trump's nominees to the MSPB.

Notes

1 However, debate over the full reach of presidential removal power continued for decades and was addressed eventually by the courts. See the cases reviewed below, including *Myers* v. *United States*, 272 U.S. 52 (1926); *Humphrey's Executor* v. *United States*, 295 U.S. 602 (1935); *Free Enterprise Fund* v. *Public Company Accounting Oversight Board*, 561 U.S. 477 (2010); and *Seila Law LLC* v. *Consumer Financial Protection Bureau*, 591 U.S. ____ (2020).

2 William McKinley's Executive Order 101 of July 27, 1897 amended what was known at the time as Section 8 of Civil Service Rule II by adding the following statement:

> No removal shall be made from any position subject to competitive examination except for just cause and upon written charges filed with the head of the Department, or other appointing officer, and of which the accused shall have full notice and an opportunity to make defense.

Theodore Roosevelt's Executive Order number 173 of May 29, 1902 further amended Section 8 of Civil Service Rule II by adding:

> Whereas certain misunderstandings have existed in regard to the proper construction of section 8 of Civil Service Rule II, which provides as follows:

> No removal shall be made from the competitive classified service except for just cause and for reasons given in writing; and the person sought to be removed shall have notice and be furnished a copy of such reasons, and be allowed a reasonable time for personally answering the same in writing. Copy of such reasons, notice, and answer and of the order of removal shall be made a part of the records of the proper department or office; and the reasons for any change in rank or compensation within the competitive classified service shall also be made a part of the records of the proper department or office.

> Now, for the purpose of preventing all such misunderstandings and improper constructions of said section, it is hereby declared that the term "just cause," as used in section 8, Civil Service Rule II, is intended to mean any cause, other than one merely political or religious, which will promote the efficiency of the service; and *nothing contained in said rule shall be construed to require the examination of witnesses or any trial or hearing except in the discretion of the officer making the removal.* (emphasis added).

The legislation known as the Lloyd–LaFollette Act of 1912 was inserted as Section 6 of HR 21279, Public Law No. 336, dated August 24, 1912, and entitled: An Act Making Appropriations for the Post Office Department and for Other Purposes. It is found in United States Statutes at Large, Vol. 37, page 555. The full text reads as follows:

> Sec. 6. That no person in the classified civil service of the United States shall be removed therefrom except for such cause as will promote the efficiency of said service and for reasons given in writing, and the person whose removal is sought shall have notice of the same and of any charges preferred against him,

and be furnished with a copy thereof, and also be allowed a reasonable time for personally answering the same in writing, and affidavits in support thereof; but no examination of witnesses nor any trial or hearing shall be required except in the discretion of the officer making the removal; and copies of charges, notice of hearing, answer, reasons for removal and of the order of removal shall be made a part of the records of the proper department or office, as shall also the reasons for reduction in rank or compensation; and copies of the same shall be furnished to the person affected upon request, and the Civil Service Commission also shall, upon request, be furnished copies of the same: Provided, however, That membership in any society, association, club, or other form of organization of postal employees not affiliated with any outside organization imposing an obligation or duty upon them to engage in any strike, or proposing to assist them in any strike, against the United States, having for its objects, among other things, improvements in the condition of labor of its members, including hours of labor and compensation therefor and leave of absence, by any person or groups of persons in said postal service, or the presenting by any such person or groups or persons of any grievance or grievances to the Congress or any Member thereof shall not constitute or be cause for reduction in rank or compensation or removal of such person or groups of persons from said service. The right of persons employed in the civil service of the United States, either individually or collectively, to petition Congress or any Member thereof, or to furnish information to either House of Congress, or to any committee or member thereof, shall not be denied or interfered with.

3 This view of civil service prevails among conservatives not only concerning the federal sector but also regarding merit systems at the state and local levels. Civil service reforms in the state of Georgia in the 1990s and in other states subsequently provide abundant evidence of this point of view. See, for example, Kim and Kellough (2014) and Nigro and Kellough (2000).

3

DISABLING THE MERIT SYSTEMS PROTECTION BOARD

The Merit Systems Protection Board (MSPB) exists to adjudicate disputes that arise between employees and their agencies over the interpretation and application of rules governing personnel management in the federal service. Disputes of this nature are bound to arise in a workforce of over two million civilian employees, and it is essential that an administrative structure be in place to resolve them. Employees who believe their agencies have treated them unfairly in violation of merit principles can file appeals with the MSPB seeking relief from prohibited personnel practices. The Board investigates complaints and works to ensure adherence to the concept of merit in the application of personnel policy. Despite the importance of this mission, however, the agency was essentially shut down during the four years of the Trump Administration. The MSPB was unable during that time to perform its central adjudicatory function. The Board was established through presidential action and legislative concurrence. It had been in operation for nearly 40 years when it was effectively disabled under President Trump.

The usual process for creating organizations within the federal government is for the U.S. Congress to establish and fund them by exercising its legislative authority. That is true for the formation of executive departments as well as the creation of independent regulatory bureaus and agencies. In the 1930s, however, there was a view among many political leaders that the President, as the Chief Executive, should occasionally share this responsibility by exercising the power to reorganize executive branch institutions. This delegation of a share of legislative authority was legally possible due to a ruling of the U.S. Supreme Court

DOI: 10.4324/9781032656380-3

in 1928 indicating that the right of Congress to delegate a share of legislative authority to the President to reorganize the executive branch was not prohibited by the Constitution as long as Congress specified an "intelligible principle" that would guide the President's action (see, *J. W. Hampton, Jr. & Co.* v. *United States*, 276 U.S. 394 (1928)).

The first example of this kind of Congressional delegation of authority came with passage of the Economy Act of 1932 (47 Stat. 413). The Act authorized presidential reorganization of the executive branch but granted Congress the authority to nullify reorganization orders within 60 days through a resolution in either House. President Herbert Hoover issued a series of reorganization plans in December of 1932 after he had lost the November election to Franklin Roosevelt. Congress vetoed all of those proposals in January of 1933, so no action was taken (Fisher, 1998; Hogue, 2012). After President Roosevelt's inauguration in 1933, Congress amended the Economy Act of 1932 to grant Roosevelt reorganization authority, and the President used that authority to make important but modest reorganizations such as establishing an Office of National Parks, Buildings, and Reservations in the Department of the Interior (Hogue, 2012). President Roosevelt requested new authority to restructure the executive branch after his reelection in 1936, and Congress responded with the Reorganization Act of 1939 (*53 Stat. 561*), which allowed Roosevelt two years to transfer, consolidate, or abolish agency or departmental functions and rename executive organizations. The Reorganization Act required that the President present his plans for reorganization to Congress and that those plans would become effective unless the House of Representatives and the Senate, in a joint resolution, registered their disapproval within 60 days (53 Stat. 562–563). In this way, Congress retained the power to veto what the President planned. Roosevelt used this delegation of authority to accomplish the first major reorganization of the federal executive branch since the founding of the government, acting in part in response to recommendations from the report of the President's Committee on Administrative Management, known more commonly as the Brownlow Committee after the name of its Chair Louis Brownlow (Hogue, 2012; Mosher, 1975).

In subsequent years, additional limited reorganization authority was granted to all Presidents from Truman through Reagan (see Hogue, 2012; Lewis, 2003; Relyea, 2008, pp. 13–14; Walker, 2003).[1] These delegations of authority all contained provisions through which Congress could veto actions proposed by a vote of one or both houses. However, in 1983, the U.S. Supreme Court invalidated the legislative veto. Instead, it required a favorable vote on legislation in both houses approving the planned reorganization and the signature of the President on that bill (see *Immigration and Naturalization Service* v. *Chadha*

(462 U.S. 919)). This ruling meant that reorganization would require ordinary Congressional legislative action. Since that time, there have been no further delegations of reorganization authority from Congress to the President.

The Carter Reforms

The presidential reform with the most direct impact on the operation of the U.S. merit system and the structure of public personnel management within the federal government occurred under President Carter. As a candidate, Carter had campaigned on the promise to reform the federal bureaucracy to make it more efficient and responsive to the American people (Arnold, 1998). Once he was elected, he pushed for reorganization authority, which was granted through the Reorganization Act of 1977 (91 Stat. 29). The law, passed in early April 1977, gave the President a three-year window in which to propose and implement any reorganization of the executive agencies, which would promote the efficiency and effectiveness of the executive branch by improving management, reducing expenditures through the coordination and consolidation of agencies and functions of government, and eliminating overlapping authorities and duplication of effort (91 Stat. 29). President Carter used his new authority to consolidate federal functions related to education into a new Department of Education. Similarly, the President grouped federal organizations dealing with diverse aspects of energy policy into a new Department of Energy. Carter also sent ten reorganization plans to Congress: two in 1977, four in 1978, three in 1979, and one in 1980 (Arnold, 1998, pp. 327–329). These plans, which all survived the legislative veto threat, addressed a wide array of issues ranging from consolidating functions in the Executive Office of the President and creating an International Communication Agency to establishing the Office of U.S. Trade Representative (Arnold, 1998, pp. 328–329). The plan that addressed the civil service and led to substantial structural reform of federal personnel management was the second Reorganization Plan of 1978.

Reorganization Plan No. 2 of 1978 was intended to correct a perceived defect in the assignment of authority to the U.S. Civil Service Commission, which had existed since its authorization in the Pendleton Act of 1883. The Civil Service Commission was responsible for establishing rules for federal personnel operations, but it was also responsible for hearing and adjudicating employee complaints that arose from the application of those rules. The President and officials in his Administration believed that those two functions (i.e., rulemaking and adjudication) should be housed in separate and independent organizations. Accordingly, Reorganization Plan No. 2 of 1978 created an Office of Personnel

Management (OPM) headed by a single Director appointed by the President with Senate confirmation. OPM was to be the government's central personnel agency responsible for establishing and enforcing merit system rules and procedures and managing employee pay and benefits – including health insurance and retirement benefits.

The remainder of the old Civil Service Commission was redesignated as the Merit Systems Protection Board, which was designed as a quasi-judicial independent agency of the federal government that would investigate and resolve complaints arising from employees regarding personnel practices. The reorganization plan also established a Federal Labor Relations Authority (FLRA) to oversee the government's labor relations policies associated with employee unions and collective bargaining. Reorganization Plan No. 2 of 1978 was placed into effect on January 1, 1979, by EO 12107 of December 28, 1978. However, legislation was needed to amend Title 5 of the U.S. Code to reflect the establishment of OPM, the MSPB, and the FLRA through Carter's reorganization. This legislative requirement was met through passage of the Civil Service Reform Act of 1978 (CSRA), which was signed into law on October 13, 1978 and became effective on January 11, 1979. The CSRA amended Title 5 of the U.S. Code in order to place Carter's reforms on a statutory basis, but also articulated an expanded list of fundamental merit principles for the federal service, specified prohibited personnel practices, and authorized the establishment of a Senior Executive Service, a merit pay plan for mid-level managers, and personnel management research and demonstration projects to explore innovative new approaches to personnel policy.

The Role of the MSPB

All of the organizations established by President Carter serve critical functions. The purpose of the MSPB is, as its name suggests, to protect core merit principles underlying the federal service. The agency accomplishes this mission by hearing complaints of violations of those principles filed by federal employees. In short, the Board ensures the continuance of a merit-based federal civil service. It provides a direct forum where federal employees may appeal agency decisions that violate merit principles. The Board may adjudicate employee appeals of adverse personnel actions such as dismissal or suspension, reductions in pay and demotion, claims of prohibited personnel actions including violations of the Hatch Act which bans certain forms of political activity by federal employees, disputes over employee benefits, and similar matters. The Board also conducts surveys of federal employees and directs other studies of the federal civil service.

The Board consists of three members appointed by the President, with Senate confirmation, for staggered seven-year terms. Under the law, no more than two members are to be from the same political party. In practice, this requirement means that the partisan balance will consist of two Board members appointed from the President's party and the third from the other party. At least two members of the Board must be present to constitute a quorum necessary for the Board to take action. A professional MSPB staff is distributed nationwide in regional and field offices and in Washington, D.C.

Any federal employee who has received an adverse personnel decision, such as a dismissal, suspension, reduction in rank, reduction in pay, or official reprimand, and wishes to appeal that decision may do so, in writing, at the MSPB regional or field office serving the area where the employee worked when the action was taken. When an appeal is filed, the MSPB assigns the case to an Administrative Judge who will issue a decision based on the evidence presented. These decisions become final unless a petition is filed requesting a review by the 3-member Board in Washington. Initial decisions by administrative judges in regional or field offices almost always support the employing agency's position. For example, in fiscal year 2016, the last full fiscal year of the Obama Administration, 8,121 appeals were received by regional or field Offices. Of that number, 3,619 were dismissed after initial review. Of the 4,502 appeals that were not dismissed, only 225 (2.7 percent of the total original appeals) resulted in the overturning or modifying of actions taken by federal agencies (U.S. Merit Systems Protection Board, 2017). According to the more recent FY 2021 Annual Report, the MSPB received 4,649 appeals from employees from October 1, 2020 through September 30, 2021. From that number, Administrative Judges dismissed 3,082 at the regional or field level, and 1,567 were reviewed. Ultimately, however, only 139 of the cases (2.9 percent of the total original appeals) resulted in the overturning or modifying of agency decisions (U.S. Merit Systems Protection Board, 2022a). These numbers, which are reported officially by the MSPB, show that nearly all initial employee appeals fail (i.e., the government agencies prevail). However, there is evidence that when we consider only the appeals of dismissals, employees are more successful. James Sherk (2022) finds that in about 28 percent of the cases, dismissals are mitigated or reversed, and back pay is frequently awarded. Consequently, there is a mixed record on rulings by the MSPB, but the vast majority of petitions for review filed by employees and received by the Board in Washington, D.C. end with the Board supporting the agencies involved.

In President Obama's second term, Board members included Susan Tsui Grundmann (a Democrat), Anne Wagner (a Democrat), and Mark Robbins (a Republican). Grundmann, who served as Chair, had worked earlier as General Counsel for the National Air Traffic Controllers Association and the National Federation of Federal Employees. She began her service on the Board in November of 2009 (U.S. Merit Systems Protection Board, 2022b). Anne Wagner served as the Board's Vice Chair. Before her appointment to the MSPB, she served as Assistant General Counsel for the American Federation of Government Employees (AFGE) and General Counsel at the Personnel Appeals Board at the Government Accountability Office. Wagner's service began in November 2009 (U.S. Merit Systems Protection Board, 2022b). Mark Robbins began his service on the Board in May of 2012. Previously, he served as the General Counsel for the U.S. Election Assistance Commission, and earlier, he had been the Executive Director of the White House Privacy and Civil Liberties Oversight Board During the George W. Bush Administration from 2006 to 2008 and General Counsel at the U.S. Office of Personnel Management from 2001 to 2006 (Judicial Nomination Commission, 2024; U.S. Merit Systems Protection Board, 2022b).

On March 1, 2015, Wagner's term on the Board ended. Her appointment had been extended by one year under the Board's enabling statute, which permits a member to remain in office for up to a year while waiting for a new member to be confirmed and sworn in to succeed them. Wagner subsequently accepted an Associate Special Counsel position at the U.S. Office of Special Counsel (a separate agency). President Obama nominated Mark Phillip Cohen to fill Wagner's position on July 8, 2015. Mr. Cohen had worked previously at the U.S. Office of Special Counsel from 2011 to 2017 and on the Board of the Government Accountability Project, a whistleblower protection and advocacy organization (HIAS, 2022). Mr. Cohen's nomination was referred to the Senate Committee on Homeland Security and Governmental Affairs chaired by Senator Ron Johnson (Republican of Wisconsin). However, the Republican-controlled Senate took no action on Mr. Cohen's nomination, and on January 3, 2017, they returned it to the President.[2] Thus, from March 1, 2015, to January 2017, the Board consisted only of Grundmann and Robbins, who were split politically; one was a Democrat and one a Republican. If they disagreed on an appeal, there was no one to break the tie, and, in those cases, the initial decision of the Administrative Judge who heard the case in the regional or field office where the complaint arose originally would remain in place.

Grundmann's service was initially scheduled to end on March 1, 2016, but her service was extended until January 7, 2017, and she left the Board on that date. Therefore, when President Trump was inaugurated on January 20, 2017,

Mark Robbins was the only member. This development meant the Board lacked a quorum and could not conduct official business. On January 23, President Trump designated Mr. Robbins as Vice Chairman. In that capacity, he continued to review cases and submitted his opinions. However, the Board's final decisions were put on hold until a quorum could be established, but the Trump Administration did not act immediately to nominate members. Mr. Robbins' term was set originally to expire on March 1, 2018. It was extended, however, for one year as the enabling statute permitted (U.S. Merit Systems Protection Board, 2022b).

On March 12, 2018, more than a year after he assumed office, President Trump sent two nominations for MSPB positions to the Senate Committee on Homeland Security and Governmental Affairs: Dennis D. Kirk to be Chair and Andrew F. Maunz to replace Mr. Robbins as Vice Chair. Both were Republicans. Kirk had been an Associate General Counsel in the Department of the Army, and Maunz had been an attorney working for the Office of General Counsel in the Social Security Administration. In that role, Maunz represented the agency in disputes arising with social security recipients or potential recipients. The President followed the Kirk and Maunz nominations with the nomination of Julia Clark, a Democrat, on June 20, 2018. At the time, Clark was Deputy General Counsel of the Congressional Office of Compliance, a congressional agency charged with the task of protecting workplace rights of employees working for the legislative branch. Earlier, she had been the General Counsel for the FLRA. The FLRA is the agency that supervises federal employee unions and collective bargaining processes (see Chapter 7, *infra*). The FLRA General Counsel is responsible for investigating claims of unfair labor practices and, when warranted, bringing cases to the members of the FLRA for final decisions.

Action/Inaction in the U.S. Senate During the Trump Years

On July 19, 2018, the Senate Committee on Homeland Security and Governmental Affairs held a hearing on the Kirk, Maunz, and Clark nominations. All three nominees expressed support for the mission of the MSPB and pledged to work to reduce the backlog of appeals that had accumulated since the Board lost its quorum in January 2017. Nevertheless, a coalition of federal employee unions submitted a letter into the record opposing the nominations of Kirk and Maunz. The unions feared those nominees would be unreceptive to employee appeals (U.S. Senate, 2018a).

The Committee scheduled a vote on the nominees on November 28, 2018. The first nominee considered was Andrew Maunz. Interestingly, the Committee, which consisted of 8 Republicans and 7 Democrats, voted 7 to 7 along party lines on Maunz (U.S. Senate, 2018b). Sen. Rand Paul (Republican from Kentucky) was not present for the vote, but Committee Chairman Ron Johnson of Wisconsin indicated that Senator Paul was voting "no" by proxy. Because "proxy" votes are recorded for the record but do not count in determining the outcome, Senator Paul's opposition did not influence the result (Ogrysko, 2018). As a result, the Committee lacked enough votes to move Maunz's nomination forward. Senate Committee Chairman Johnson then decided not to call for a confirmation vote for the other nominees (Kirk and Clark) until the Committee agreed to clear Maunz. With that decision by Senator Johnson, the confirmation process was effectively stopped (Katz, 2018). Because no action was taken, the nominations of Kirk, Maunz, and Clark were returned to the President when the 115th Congress adjourned on January 3, 2019.

On January 16, 2019, President Trump resubmitted the three nominations for reconsideration by the Senate Committee on Homeland Security and Governmental Affairs in the 116th Congress's first session. At this time, because of changes in the makeup of the Senate following the 2018 election, the Committee consisted of eight Republicans and six Democrats (Joint Committee on Printing, 2020). But on February 12, the day before the Committee was scheduled to vote, Maunz withdrew his nomination in response to continued union opposition. The other nominees, Kirk and Clark, were approved by the Committee on February 13, 2019 (U.S. Senate, 2019a). Before the vote, Senator Paul indicated he would vote "no," not because of opposition to the nominees but because of his opposition to the MSPB itself. In explaining his position, Senator Paul said that he opposed the Board as a matter of principle and argued that the MSPB had "morphed into job protection, not really merit evaluation" (Ogrysko, 2019a; U.S. Senate, 2019a). This position is interesting, given the data on MSPB rulings reviewed earlier, showing that the actions taken by federal agencies are almost always upheld with the possible exception of cases involving appeals of dismissals.

On March 1, 2019, Mark Robbins' term on the MSPB expired. Committee Chair Senator Johnson declined to send the Kirk and Clark nominations to the floor of the Senate, where their confirmation would have produced a tied Board consisting of one Republican and one Democrat. Senator Johnson argued that he would wait until the President named a third nominee. According to Deborah Hopkins, a federal employment attorney in Washington D.C., Johnson claimed, "It's typical that all nominees get voted on together in the full Senate" (Hopkins, 2019).

However, as Hopkins points out, "the MSPB members intentionally have staggered terms, and ... we have never had all three members voted on at the same time" (Hopkins, 2019). According to Hopkins, Senator Johnson's statement and refusal to move the nominees forward raised the question of whether he was following an "intentional strategy to keep the Board vacant or it was a simple misunderstanding" (Hopkins, 2019). It is possible that Senator Johnson and other Republicans preferred a vacant Board to one with only one Republican and one Democrat. A Board with that composition would have the quorum needed to conduct business, but because of the equal party divide, the reversal of Board policy developed under eight years of the Obama Presidency could not be achieved as the Republicans wished. Senator Johnson withheld the Kirk and Clark nominations from the Senate floor, and the MSPB was completely vacant after Robins departed. Senator Johnson's decision not to push for confirmation of Kirk and Clark effectively shut down the final administrative arbiter for employee appeals of personnel actions. For the first time since the Board's creation, there were no members (Ogrysko, 2019b).

The Senate Committee on Homeland Security and Governmental Affairs continued to hold the nominations of Kirk and Clark as it waited for a third presidential nominee. On April 30, 2019, the President responded by nominating Republican Chad Bungard. Bungard was Deputy Counsel for the Office of Analytics, Review, and Oversight at the Social Security Administration and had also served as General Counsel for the MSPB under President George W. Bush. The nomination of Bungard, along with those of Kirk and Clark, would have filled the Board and allowed it to address the backlog of pending appeals (Ogrysko 2019c).

A hearing was held on June 12, 2019, to consider Bungard's nomination (U.S. Senate, 2019b), and he was unanimously approved by the Committee on June 19, 2019 (Katz, 2019; U.S. Senate, 2019c). The Republican Senate then moved to confirm all three MSPB nominees with a single vote through unanimous consent. But under unanimous consent, if any Senator objects, even privately, the vote cannot go forward. That is apparently what happened. While no senator publicly objected to any of the candidates, the Senate took no action, and the Board was allowed to remain vacant through the remainder of 2019 and all of 2020 (Ogrysko, 2020). Appeals to the Board continued to accumulate. By the end of 2020, there were 3,071 appeals awaiting review (Ogrysko, 2021a).

On January 3, 2021, the Kirk, Clark, and Bungard nominations were returned to the President. President Trump immediately re-nominated Dennis Kirk. But importantly, following the runoff election on January 5, 2021 for Georgia's two seats in the U.S. Senate and the victories of Democrats Raphael

Warnock and Jon Ossoff, the Democratic party gained control of the Senate by the slimmest of margins. On February 4th, the new President, President Biden, withdrew Kirk's nomination.

Action under the Biden Administration

President Biden nominated Cathy A. Harris to Chair the Board and Raymond Limon to be a member on June 24, 2021. Both Harris and Limon were Democrats. Harris had worked as an Assistant District Attorney in Manhattan and more recently as an attorney specializing in federal employment law in a Washington D.C. law firm. Limon served as the Chief Human Capital Officer for the Department of the Interior and had also worked on human resources management matters at the State Department and OPM (Ogrysko, 2021b). Biden followed these nominations with the nomination of Tristan Leavitt, a Republican, on September 13, 2021. At the time of his nomination, Leavitt was working as the General Counsel at the MSPB and had been the agency's de facto director since March 2019 (Ogrysko, 2021c).

The Committee on Homeland Security and Governmental Affairs, now chaired by Democrat Gary C. Peters of Michigan, held a hearing on Biden's three nominees on September 22, 2021 (U.S. Senate, 2021). Harris faced opposition from Republican Senators who expressed concern over messages she had posted on social media that were overtly partisan, but no opposition was expressed regarding Limon and Leavitt (Katz, 2021; U.S. Senate, 2021). The Limon and Leavitt nominations were reported favorably out of the Committee on October 6, 2021. No action was taken on the Harris nomination, and at the end of the 117th Congress, First Session on January 3, 2022, her nomination was returned to the President. Biden re-nominated Harris the next day, and her nomination was referred back to the Senate Committee on Homeland Security and Governmental Affairs. The Senate had held the nominations of Limon and Leavitt over to the 117th Congress, Second Session, and they were confirmed by voice vote in the Senate on March 1, 2022 (U.S. Senate, 2022). In this case, the procedure simply required that the nominations be presented to the Senate so that those Senators who were present could register their support or opposition by saying "yea" or "nay." The presiding officer would then announce the results according to his or her best judgment. The Harris nomination was reported favorably out of the Committee on February 2, 2022, but because of lingering opposition, her confirmation was delayed until May 25, 2022 and was achieved through a roll-call vote along party lines with 48 yes votes and 46 no votes (U.S. Senate, 2022).

How should we understand the unfortunate saga of the MSPB during the Trump years? Clearly, the story illustrates the deep partisan divide prevalent then and now. Senator Johnson's refusal to move the nominations of Kirk and Clark forward until President Trump named a third nominee produced unnecessary delay. There was no tradition or committee precedent of sending three Board nominees together to the Senate floor, as Johnson argued, since their terms are staggered and do not expire simultaneously, and the Committee had never been in the position of reviewing three nominees simultaneously. Even when the MSPB was originally established and the first nominations were sent forward, only two were considered in January 1979. The Senate confirmed the third in October of 1979 (U.S. Merit Systems Protection Board, 2022d). Senator Johnson apparently preferred no functioning Board to one unable to shift policy in the direction preferred by Republicans.

Eventually, the third Trump nominee was named and approved by the Senate committee. At that point, one could be tempted to argue that the Republicans' insistence on unanimous consent for confirmation of President Trump's nominees before the full Senate was designed to derail the approval process, especially when it is contrasted with how President Biden's nominees were handled. There is, nevertheless, no evidence to support that conclusion. There was no partisan advantage to Republicans in keeping the Board vacant after three nominees were available. Indeed, they would be advantaged by a functioning Board with a Republican majority. Furthermore, unanimous consent is frequently used to enable the Senate to manage its heavy workload. Time on the Senate floor must be limited given the volume of business handled, including the thousands of nominations to be considered. The mechanism of unanimous consent enables the Senate to manage its affairs expeditiously, and typically, multiple questions for which unanimous consent is requested are bundled together through a process of negotiation designed to ensure success. Obviously, that process failed in this case, and no MSPB members were confirmed during the four years of the Trump Presidency. At a minimum, one can conclude from this experience that filling positions on the MSPB was not an issue sufficiently high on the Republican agenda to compel them to employ a strategy to ensure confirmation. At worst, the action gave the Trump Administration greater flexibility in managing employees free from concern for employee complaints. As noted previously, agency actions were almost always upheld by the Board, but the appeals process took time. Thus, the MSPB was essentially disabled. The ability of the Board to hear appeals alleging prohibited personnel actions, as it was originally intended to do, was halted during the four years of the Trump Presidency.

Notes

1 Since the 1930s, Presidents have also occasionally acted on existing constitutional or statutory authority to create new agencies via executive order. Presidents and Cabinet Secretaries also sometimes act on the basis of vague statutes to establish sub-agencies and bureaus. Specific delegations of authority from Congress to the President may also be the basis for presidential action to establish agencies. See, Lewis (2003, pp. 78–80).

2 Information on all nominations made to the MSPB and the actions taken by the Senate Committee on Homeland Security and Governmental Affairs is retrieved from the Congress.Gov website under nominations for the requisite session of Congress. For example, information on the Mark Cohen nomination is found at: https://www.congress.gov/nomination/114th-congress/634/actions?s=3&r=20&overview=closed

4

TRUMP'S EXECUTIVE ORDERS ON FEDERAL LABOR RELATIONS

Presidential executive orders are directives or commands issued by the President requiring specific actions regarding organizational structure or policy implementation within the executive branch. These orders are released under presidential authority grounded in Article 2 of the U.S. Constitution, prior legislative authorizations, or both. Nearly all presidents have relied on executive orders to direct government operations. William Henry Harrison is the exception; since he died after only one month in office (he served from March 4, 1841 to April 4, 1841), he issued no executive orders.[1] Many presidents, especially those in the Republic's earliest decades, issued very few. President Washington issued eight orders, but Presidents John Adams, James Madison, and James Monroe each issued only one. President Franklin Roosevelt holds the record for the most executive orders, issuing 3,728 during his more than 12 years in office. Other presidents also issued many executive orders, including President Woodrow Wilson with 1,803, Calvin Coolidge with 1,203, and Theodore Roosevelt with 1,081. In more recent years, less than 200 executive orders were issued each presidential term. President George W. Bush, for example, issued 173 in his first term and 118 in his second term, while President Obama issued 148 in his first term and 129 in his second.[2] The label "executive order" was not applied to presidential directives until President Lincoln issued orders, and the sequential numbering system used today began with an order issued by Lincoln in October of 1862 (Relyea, 2008).

President Trump issued 220 executive orders during his four years in office, a number only slightly larger than that of other recent presidents. In addition, as is true

DOI: 10.4324/9781032656380-4

of other presidents, Trump's orders addressed a wide range of issues. Many were designed to reduce federal regulations on businesses or to promote border security. Others addressed topics such as federal assistance for state and local law enforcement, efforts to strengthen cyber security, and programs to enhance the efficiency of federal agency operations, to name only a few. Directly relevant to the issues addressed in this book, however, several of President Trump's Executive Orders addressed the operation of the U.S. civil service.

Disbanding Labor–Management Forums

One of President Trump's first orders, number 13812, issued on September 29, 2017, revoked an executive order issued by President Obama creating a National Council on Federal Labor–Management Relations and Labor–Management Forums within individual federal agencies (see Obama's order 13522 of December 9, 2009). The National Council established by Obama consisted of the Director of the Office of Personnel Management (OPM), the Deputy Director for Management of the Office of Management and Budget (OMB), the Federal Labor Relations Authority Chair, and the presidents of federal employee unions and associations. The purpose was to reinstate a policy that originated under President Clinton to facilitate labor–management cooperation in the federal civil service by promoting non-adversarial discussions of "workplace challenges and problems" and to work cooperatively to develop solutions to those problems and facilitate cooperative collective bargaining processes within the federal executive branch (see Executive Order 13522). Clinton's program of labor–management cooperation had been terminated by President George W. Bush on February 17, 2001 through Executive Order 13203. Obama's National Council was to support the reinstatement of Labor–Management Forums within federal departments and agencies to advance further understanding and cooperation between federal employee unions and management. Thus, the existence of these mechanisms to promote cooperation between labor and management in the federal service swung like a pendulum between Republican and Democratic Presidential Administrations. They were in place when Democrats were in office and were out of favor under Republicans. While it took some time for Obama's program to become fully operational, by 2014, federal employee union officials were generally happy with the initiative. They indicated they had more voice in agency decision-making processes (Moore, 2014). It is likely, however, that the success of agency-level Labor–Management Forums varied depending on the level of support registered by agency leadership and commitment from union leaders.[3]

The Trump Administration approached organized labor and federal employee unions from a perspective decidedly different from that of Obama. President Trump's Order argued that "The National Council on Federal Labor-Management Relations (Council) and related agency-level Labor-Management Forums have consumed considerable managerial time and taxpayer resources, but they have not fulfilled their goal of promoting collaboration in the Federal workforce" (Executive Order 13812, September 29, 2017). Accordingly, the President required all "rules, regulations, guidelines, programs, or policies" developed through the work of the National Council on Federal Labor–Management Relations or Labor–Management Forums within individual federal agencies be rescinded (Executive Order 13812, September 29, 2017).

On Wednesday, March 6, 2024, President Biden issued an Executive Order reinstituting Labor–Management Forums to promote cooperation between federal agencies and the unions representing their employees. The new Order argued that "Labor-Management Forums provide an opportunity for managers, employees, and employees' union representatives to discuss how Federal Government operations can promote satisfactory labor relations and improve the productivity and effectiveness of the Federal Government." In short, President Biden argued that Labor-Management Forums would promote the development of "cooperative and productive labor-management relations."

Constraining Employees and Their Unions

On May 25, 2018, President Trump issued two Executive Orders, numbered 13836 and 13837, limiting federal employee union activities. One of President Biden's first acts when he took office was to rescind these orders. Nevertheless, they collectively illustrated ways in which presidential prerogatives may shape the federal personnel system and employee rights within that system.

Executive Order 13836 was entitled "Developing Efficient, Effective, and Cost-Reducing Approaches to Federal Sector Collective Bargaining." This Order is hereafter referred to as the "Collective Bargaining Order." Section 1 of the Order argues that implementation of the Federal Service Labor–Management Relations Statute (Title VII of the Civil Service Reform Act of 1978) has not been accomplished in a manner "consistent with the requirement [in the law] of an effective and efficient Government" (Federal Register, 2018a, p. 25329). Indeed, the Order asserts that collective bargaining agreements "often make it harder for agencies to reward high performers, hold low performers accountable, or flexibly respond to operational needs" (Federal Register, 2018a, p. 25329).

The basis for these claims is not specified. However, they are popular in Republican circles and are derived from the difficulties many agencies have experienced in disciplining or removing employees who engage in misconduct or those whose performance is otherwise unacceptable. Under existing law that traces back to the McKinley and Theodore Roosevelt Executive Orders noted in Chapter 2, the Lloyd–LaFollette Act of 1912, and Supreme Court precedent (*Cleveland Board of Education* v. *Loudermill*), employees in the classified service must be given notice prior to dismissal and an opportunity to explain the behavior that has led to the pending dismissal. This process slows termination proceedings, but it is not the only difficulty encountered. Employees have a right to appeal after dismissal, and those appeals are frequently successful. Appeals may go to the Merit Systems Protection Board, where, as we have seen, removals are mitigated or reversed (often with back pay) about 28 percent of the time (Sherk, 2022). But more importantly, when employees are in unionized settings, dismissals may be reviewed through a grievance process where a neutral arbitrator will adjudicate the case. In these instances, employees successfully get their jobs back approximately 54 percent of the time and are often awarded back pay (Sherk, 2022). The Collective Bargaining Order sets out new procedures and requirements for federal collective bargaining that are partly motivated by a desire to address these kinds of issues.

The first new requirement (detailed in Section 3 of the Order) is the establishment of an "Interagency Labor Relations Working Group." This group would consist of the Director of OPM and representatives from each participating agency. All agencies with at least 1,000 employees represented by a federal union were required to join the group, and agencies with smaller numbers of employees represented by unions were permitted to participate at the discretion of the head of the agency and the OPM Director. The purpose of the group was, among other things, to develop:

> model ground rules for negotiations that, if implemented, would minimize delay, set reasonable limits for good-faith negotiations, call for [the] Federal Mediation and Conciliation Service (FMCS) to mediate disputed issues not resolved within a reasonable time, and, as appropriate, promptly bring remaining unresolved issues to the Federal Services Impasses Panel (the Panel) for resolution.
>
> *Federal Register (2018a, p. 25330)*

Other important provisions of the Order include Section 5 (a), which mandated "a negotiating period of 6 weeks or less to achieve ground rules [for bargaining], and a negotiating period of between 4 and 6 months" to final-ize a contract (Federal Register, 2018a, p. 25330). President Trump apparently believed that six months should be sufficient. That conclusion was, no doubt, a reaction to the fact that there are times when negotiations have dragged on for years. One example of this kind of extended negotiating period is the widely observed dispute in negotiations between the Trump Administration and the American Federation of Government Employees (AFGE) over a contract for employees in the Veterans Administration. The dispute lasted over six years and stretched into the Biden Presidency, which settled it in August of 2023 (Wagner, 2023). Part of Trump's Collective Bargaining Order (Section 5 (e)) specified that during negotiations, agency representatives must request the ex-change of written proposals to facilitate negotiations and permit the agency to assess the potential impact of the union's proposals on "agency operations and management rights" (Federal Register, 2018a, p. 25332). Finally, Section 6 prohibits agencies from bargaining over subjects identified in the law as issues on which bargaining is permitted but not mandatory. These subjects include "the numbers, types, and grades of employees or positions assigned to any organizational subdivision, work project, or tour of duty, or on the technology, methods, and means of performing work" (Title 5, U.S. Code Section 7106 (b) (1)).

The next order, Executive Order 13837, was entitled "Ensuring Transpar-ency, Accountability, and Efficiency in Taxpayer-Funded Union Time Use." This Order is hereafter referred to as the "Official Time Order." Under the federal collective bargaining statute, federal employees holding official posi-tions within their unions may conduct union duties while at work. The purpose of this Executive Order from Trump was to restrict the time union officials could devote to these activities. Time spent on union activities by employees who hold union positions is generally referred to as "union time" or "official time." The Order states that the President aims to promote an "effective and efficient government." In line with that purpose, the document declares that "executive branch employees should spend their duty hours performing the work of the Federal government and serving the public" (Federal Register, 2018b, p. 25335). The Official Time Order then specifies a limit on union time that can be considered "reasonable, necessary, and in the public interest" and announces that the "union time rate" must not exceed 1 hour per fiscal year for each employee within a bargaining unit (see Section 3 (a)). Under this requirement, for example, if a bargaining unit has 100 employees, union of-ficial time would be limited to 100 hours in a fiscal year. The limitation on of-ficial time was based on rates reported for the Departments of Defense, State, and Interior in a report from OPM for fiscal year 2016 (U.S. Office of Personnel Management, 2018). The Order also prohibits employees from engaging in lobbying activities while on the job and, importantly, prohibits employees who are union representatives from using government property or other agency resources free of charge, including "office or meeting space, reserved parking spaces, phones, computers, and computer systems," unless such resources are also made available to other employees acting on behalf of other non-governmental organizations (Federal Register, 2018b, p. 25337). Finally, the Order stipulates that employees may only use union time with prior written authorization from their agencies.

Streamlining Removal Procedures

A third Executive Order, of May 25, 2018, number 13839, outlined new procedures to simplify actions required to terminate federal employees. The Order was entitled "Promoting Accountability and Streamlining Removal Procedures Consistent with Merit System Principles" and is hereafter referred to as the "Removal Procedures Order." The Order declared that "Merit system principles call for holding Federal employees accountable for performance and conduct." However, the Order contended that the current civil service system has failed to meet that responsibility and cited evidence from OPM's Federal Employee Viewpoint Survey that had "consistently found that less than one-third of Federal employees believe that the Government deals with poor performers effectively" (Federal Register, 2018c, p. 25343). The Removal Procedures Order further argued that "Failure to address unacceptable performance and misconduct undermines morale, burdens good performers with subpar colleagues, and inhibits the ability of executive agencies ... to accomplish their missions" (Federal Register, 2018c, p. 25343). Section 2 (a) of the Order states that "Removing unacceptable performers should be a straightforward process that minimizes the burden on supervisors" (Federal Register, 2018c, p. 25343). With this objective in mind, the Order specified 15 changes to employee termination procedures outlined in Table 4.1.

Many of the requirements specified in Table 4.1 appear reasonable and well within the scope of presidential power. Several reflect practices already used in the federal service when the Order was issued. Nevertheless, other requirements imposed significant changes. Among those provisions are the limit of 30 days for employees to demonstrate improved performance, the prohibition on subjecting disputes over employee terminations, performance ratings, and incentive pay to grievance procedures, and the requirement that agencies maintain all information on adverse actions in employee personnel files.

TABLE 4.1 Major Provisions of Executive Order 13389 Regarding Termination Procedures

1.	The period of time given to employees to demonstrate improved performance should not exceed 30 days.
2.	Supervisors are not required to use progressive discipline.
3.	Agencies are not prohibited from removing an employee simply because they did not remove a different employee for comparable conduct.
4.	Suspension should not be a substitute for removal in circumstances in which removal would be appropriate.
5.	When taking disciplinary action, agencies should have discretion to take into account an employee's disciplinary record and past work record, including all past misconduct.
6.	Agencies should issue decisions on proposed removals within 15 business days of the end of the employee reply period following a notice of proposed removal.
7.	Agencies should limit the written notice of adverse action to the 30 days prescribed by law in Title 5, U.S. Code.
8.	The removal procedures set out in Title 5, U.S. Code, should be followed.
9.	Employees should be initially hired into a probationary period, during which time their suitability for continued employment should be assessed.
10.	Performance should be prioritized over length of service.
11.	Agencies should not enter into collective bargaining agreements that allow disputes over employee terminations to be addressed under negotiated grievance procedures.
12.	Grievance procedures may not be used to address employee disputes over performance ratings or incentive pay.
13.	Agencies shall not make any agreement, including a collective bargaining agreement, that limits the agency's discretion to engage in disciplinary procedures.
14.	Agencies shall not agree to erase, remove, alter, or withhold from another agency any information about a civilian employee's performance or conduct in that employee's Official Personnel Folder.
15.	Agencies shall report all adverse actions taken against employees to the Director of OPM.

Source: Executive Order 13839 (Federal Register, 2018, pp. 25343–25345).

The Union Response

Collectively, the President's Executive Orders from May 25, 2018 (Orders 13836, 13837, and 13839) presented a significant challenge to federal employee unions, and the unions wasted no time in taking up that challenge. Several organizations filed or later joined lawsuits in the Federal District Court for the District of Columbia. The unions involved were the National Treasury Employees Union (NTEU), the AFGE, and a coalition of 13 unions led by the National Federation of Federal Employees (NFFE).[4] Judge Ketanji Brown Jackson (now Justice Jackson of the U.S. Supreme Court) consolidated and heard the cases.

The unions' legal challenges claimed, among other things, that President Trump's Executive Orders violated aspects of the federal statute governing collective bargaining and labor relations in the federal sector (Title VII of the Civil Service Reform Act of 1978, known as the Federal Service Labor–Management Relations Statute or FSLMRS). From the unions' perspective, the Collective Bargaining Order exceeded the President's authority and violated the FSLMRS by altering the collective bargaining process by, among other things, setting time limits on negotiations, requiring the exchange of written bargaining proposals, and prohibiting negotiation on issues that are listed as permissive in the statute. The unions also argued that the Official Time Order violated the FSLMRS by restricting the use of official time in ways the statute did not permit, and the Removal Procedures Order violated the FSLMRS by establishing a 30-day limit on the time that poor-performing employees would have to demonstrate improved performance.

The Trump Administration offered two core arguments. First, from their view, the U.S. District Court lacked jurisdiction to hear the case. The FSLMRS, as established by Congress, provides an administrative dispute resolution process in which disagreements arising over labor–management relations issues would be heard by the Federal Labor Relations Authority (FLRA). Subsequent appeals of decisions of the FLRA were to go to the Federal Court of Appeals for the District of Columbia Circuit. The Administration argued that the issues raised by the unions fell clearly within the jurisdiction of the FLRA. Second, the Administration argued on the merits that the orders issued by President Trump were firmly within his authority as head of the federal executive branch. The defense cited the U.S. Supreme Court decision from 1974 in *Old Dominion Branch* v. *Austin* (418 U.S. 264), where President Nixon's Executive Order 11491 of 1969 regulating federal labor relations was upheld. The Court found in that case that Title 5 of the U.S. Code, Section 7301, gave the President power to "prescribe regulations for the conduct of employees in the executive branch." Furthermore, the Court reasoned as recently as 2010 in *Free Enterprise Fund* v. *Public Company Accounting Oversight Board* (561 U. S. 477) that "If any power whatsoever is in its nature executive, it is the power of appointing, overseeing, and controlling those who execute the laws," and that "Article II (of the U.S. Constitution) makes a single President responsible for the actions of the Executive Branch." In addition, neither the Civil Service Reform Act overall nor Title VII of that Act (the FSLMRS) divested the President of any authority over the executive branch that was held prior to enactment of the statute.

Judge Jackson, in an expedited ruling issued on August 25, 2018, agreed that the President possessed the authority to issue orders regarding federal labor–management relations but that some specific provisions of the orders issued on May 25, 2018, conflicted with the language of the federal labor relations statute and Congressional intent, and accordingly, those provisions were overturned. Among the invalidated provisions were the following:

- The provision limiting the negotiating period for "ground rules" to six weeks or less and the period for contract agreement to four to six months.
- The requirement that written proposals be exchanged between the government and the unions during negotiations.
- The prohibition of negotiation on "permissive items" as allowed under the labor relations statute.
- The limitations on the use of "official time" by union officers to perform union work while on the job and the requirement of advance written notice of use of "official time."
- The prohibition on the use of government office space and equipment for union purposes by employees holding union positions.
- The 30-day limit on the time that poor-performing employees have to demonstrate improved performance.
- The exclusion from grievance procedures of disputes over employee termination.
- The exclusion from grievance procedures or binding arbitration of disputes over employee performance ratings and the awarding of incentive pay.

Following this ruling, the Department of Justice immediately appealed to the United States Court of Appeals for the District of Columbia. In that appeal, the Administration reiterated the arguments they had made earlier that the disputes made by the unions should have been directed to the FLRA rather than to the District Court, and on the merits, the President had ample authority to issue the contested Orders regarding collective bargaining procedures, the use of official time, and removal procedures, and those Executive Orders did not violate provisions of the Federal Service Labor–Management Relations Statute. On July 16, 2019, the Appeals Court overturned Judge Jackson's ruling. Notably, rather than ruling that Judge Jackson's interpretation of the federal labor relations statute was incorrect, the Court of Appeals agreed with the Trump Administration that the District Court lacked jurisdiction to rule on the merits of the case.

According to the Court of Appeals, the unions should have taken their challenges of the President's Executive Orders first to the Federal Labor Relations Authority, the agency established by law to oversee federal labor issues and resolve disputes. However, when the cases regarding the President's Orders were filed with the District Court, the Office of General Counsel in the FLRA was vacant. That vacancy was important because it closed off one avenue by which the unions could file a complaint of unfair labor practices regarding the Trump Orders. Ordinarily, a complaint could go to the Office of General Counsel and then to an Administrative Law Judge for adjudication, and, if needed, a subsequent appeal to the FLRA could be filed. The decision by the FLRA could then be appealed to the Circuit Court of Appeals for the District of Columbia.

However, the unions could also file grievances over alleged unfair labor practices contained within the Trump Orders, and arbitrators would hear those grievances. This method of proceeding was available to the unions even though the Office of General Counsel was vacant. But it was a process that could be lengthy and time-consuming. Consequently, the unions sought more immediate assistance from the District Court. Interestingly, the Office of Special Counsel at the FLRA had been vacant since November 2017, and it remained vacant until President Biden appointed an acting General Counsel on March 24, 2021 (Wagner, 2021). By then, a backlog of approximately 450 cases was pending before the Special Counsel. President Trump had nominated an attorney to fill the position in April 2019, but the Republican-controlled Senate could not move the nomination through on unanimous consent because of opposition from employee unions and Democratic Senators.

The dispute over President Trump's Executive Orders from May 25, 2018, regarding collective bargaining, union official time, and streamlined employee removal procedures, and the court case that followed their issuance, raise important issues that are central to questions about the balance of power between the President and Congress regarding control of the federal workforce and personnel management policy. This dispute was, and is, essentially about the power of the President to direct federal collective bargaining and the ability of Congress to limit that power through statutory provisions such as those within the FSLMRS. Because presidential authority over the federal civil service rests on Article II of the U.S. Constitution, one may question whether the FSLMRS portion of the Civil Service Reform Act of 1978 is constitutional since it constrains presidential authority.[5] As discussed earlier, the U.S. Constitution, in Article II, Section 1, vests federal executive authority in the President. In addition, Article II, Section 3 states that the President "shall take care that the laws be faithfully executed." The U.S. Supreme Court has ruled that the constitutional grant of executive authority to the President confers all executive authority, not merely a portion of it, and that executive authority includes the power to direct the actions of executive branch organizations and their employees (see, *Free Enterprise Fund* v. *Public Company Accounting Oversight Board*, 561 U.S. 477 and *Seila Law LLC* v. *the Consumer Financial Protection Bureau*, 591 U.S. ____, 2020; 140 S. Ct. 2183). Given this constitutional structure regarding presidential authority, one may at a minimum ask how it is that Congress has authority to delegate power to public employees and their unions to help shape the management of executive branch organizations. One should note, however, that the Federal Labor Relations Authority, the organization that oversees federal labor relations and sits at the center of the FSLMRS was established by President Carter in his Reorganization Plan No. 2 of 1978. Thus, the framework for federal sector labor–management relations originated in presidential action.

Other Orders

President Trump issued four other executive orders addressing the federal civil service, which are worthy of discussion. One of these was Executive Order 13842 from July 10, 2018. This Order exempted certain employees of the U.S. Marshals Service, specifically Deputy U.S. Marshals and Criminal Investigators, from Competitive Selection and the classified or competitive civil service. The U.S. Marshals Service is the nation's oldest federal law enforcement agency. It is located within the Department of Justice and performs roles including "protection of the federal judiciary and federal witnesses, apprehension of federal fugitives, management and disposal of seized and forfeited properties, transportation of prisoners and hundreds of other special operations" (U.S. House of Representatives, House Report 105-27, March 17, 1997). President Trump's Executive Order regarding the Marshals Service argued that moving selected positions out of the classified civil service would "enable the USMS to be competitive in recruiting high-quality Deputy U.S. Marshals and Criminal Investigators, to better hire and retain qualified individuals in certain duty locations, and to more expeditiously fill vacant positions consistent with law enforcement needs" (Federal Register, July 13, 2018, p. 32753). The Order defended the move by saying that "it is impracticable to hold open competition or to apply usual competitive examining procedures for those positions related to Federal law enforcement" (Federal Register, July 13, 2018, p. 32753). These positions were reassigned by presidential directive to Schedule B in the Excepted Service.[6] As a result, the positions were removed from the classified civil service and merit system procedures. Even though Executive Order 13842 produced a significant change for Deputy U.S. Marshals and Criminal Investigators that arguably made their selection more flexible, the Order received little attention in the press and remained in effect during the Biden Administration.

Another order, Executive Order 13932, of June 26, 2020, was entitled "Modernizing and Reforming the Assessment and Hiring of Federal Job Candidates" (Federal Register, July 1, 2020, p. 39457). This Order required OPM and federal departments and agencies to reduce their reliance on post-secondary educational requirements (undergraduate and graduate degrees) when setting employment qualifications. The Order argues that "Federal Government employment opportunities should be filled based on merit. Policies or practices that undermine public confidence in the hiring process undermine confidence in both the civil service and the Government" (Federal Register, July 1, 2020, p. 39457). However, the Order continues by arguing that "an overreliance on college degrees excludes capable candidates and undermines labor-market efficiencies" (Federal Register, July 1, 2020, p. 39457). Specifically, the Order requires the replacement of "degree-based hiring with skills-and competency-based hiring and will hold the civil service to a higher standard – ensuring that the individuals most capable of performing the roles and responsibilities required of a specific position are those hired for that position – that is more in line with the principles on which the merit system rests" (Federal Register, July 1, 2020, p. 39458). Educational requirements are to be used only when they are legally required in the state or locality where the job is located. Federal agencies work with OPM to assess the qualifications of job candidates by reviewing their actual "knowledge, skills, competencies, and abilities" without relying on educational attainment as a measure of suitability for employment. While these requirements created significant new work for OPM and federal agencies, they are reasonable and rational. Perhaps as a result, as of February of 2024, President Trump's successor, President Biden, had not revoked the Order. To the contrary, the Biden Administration has embraced this new approach.

Two other Executive Orders from President Trump had substantial implications for the federal merit system. The first is Executive Order 13843 of July 10, 2018, which exempted Administrative Law Judges from the competitive service. This Order was a response to the decision by the U.S. Supreme Court in *Lucia v. Securities and Exchange Commission* (585 U.S. _____ 2018) finding that Administrative Law Judges are "Officers of the United States and are subject to the Constitution's Appointments Clause." The second Order, arguably the most significant, was Executive Order 13957, which created a new category in the Excepted Service for all federal employees with responsibilities related to the formation of public policy. This employment category was identified as "Schedule F." It is addressed in Chapter 6, *infra.*

Notes

1 This paragraph uses information on presidents and their executive orders from the website POTUS.com, which can be accessed at https://potus.com/presidential-facts/executive-orders/.

2 *Federal Register*, Executive Orders, accessed at: https://www.federalregister.gov/presidential-documents/executive-orders.

3 This point is made in an informative white paper produced in 2010 by Marick F. Masters of Wayne State University, Christina Sickles Merchant of the Maxwell School at Syracuse University, and Robert Tobias of American University. Their report was entitled *Engaging Federal Employees Through Their Union Representatives to Improve Agency Performance*. See Masters, Merchant, and Tobias (2010).

4 The NTEU initially filed suit in the Eastern District of Virginia but later dropped that suit and filed to join the lawsuit filed by AFGE in the D.C. District Court.

5 Howard (2017) raises similar questions about public sector collective bargaining and Congressional infringement on the power of the presidency.

6 The Excepted Service includes federal employees employed outside the classified service who are exempt from standard merit system rules governing competitive selection. Chapter 6 of this work discusses the excepted service in full.

5

THE EFFORT TO DISMANTLE OPM

On April 7, 1978, James L. Sundquist, a Brookings Institution scholar and au-
thor of several influential books on politics and public policy, provided testimony at a hearing on Reorganization Plan No. 2 of 1978 and the Civil Service
Reform Act of 1978 before the U.S. Senate Committee on Governmental Affairs.
Mr. Sundquist was then the Vice-Chair of a panel appointed by the National
Academy of Public Administration (NAPA) to develop recommendations on
President Carter's Civil Service Reform Proposals. The NAPA panel was supportive of the proposed reforms and provided a detailed assessment. One of the
first points Sundquist made was the following:

> The President, who has the Constitutional responsibility of executing the
> laws, must have the means to exercise leadership over the government's
> personnel system through an organization responsible to him.
>
> *U.S. Senate (1978, p. 393)*

Few informed observers would disagree with the sentiment expressed in that
statement, but today there is significant disagreement over what it may imply for
the federal civil service. Reorganization Plan No. 2 of 1978 (and the Civil Service
Reform Act of 1978) strengthened presidential leadership by establishing a new
central personnel office (the U.S. Office of Personnel Management or OPM)
headed by a single Director appointed by the President with the advice and consent
of the Senate. In the earlier system, which dated from the Pendleton Act of 1883,
personnel policy was established and implemented by a three-member, bi-partisan

DOI: 10.4324/9781032656380-5

Civil Service Commission with two members typically from the President's political party. The Commission structure erected a shield between the formation and implementation of personnel policy and the president. Presidential control was not as direct or immediate as it would otherwise be. By contrast, the creation of OPM led by a single director serving at the pleasure of the President placed personnel policy more directly within the reach of presidential authority.

The creation of OPM in 1978 had bipartisan support, but that did not mean then, and does not mean today that there was or is partisan agreement on the structure and operation of the federal civil service. For example, while acknowledging the President's executive authority, Democrats typically support the federal personnel system's emphasis on employee rights to procedural due process, which delay removal procedures, but which the Democrats see generally as a means of guaranteeing fairness in instances of termination or other adverse actions. Conversely, Republicans, as we have seen, favor a more expansive view of presidential control over the executive branch consistent with the Unitary Executive Theory.

The Trump Administration and Federal Reorganization

Drawing on the conservative Republican view of government and appending to that a heavy measure of nationalism and populism, Donald Trump campaigned for the Presidency in 2016 against what he argued was a wide range of federal policy failures in international trade, immigration, and regulatory policy. Candidate Trump bemoaned what he described as excessive federal regulations and inefficiencies in federal management. Steve Bannon, a chief strategist and campaign director for Trump, argued that Trump would push for the "deconstruction of the administrative state" (Rucker and Costa, 2017). Indeed, Trump often cast himself as the chief combatant in a struggle against a "deep state" consisting of personnel and institutions in the executive branch intent on opposing leadership by duly elected chief executives (Skowronek, Dearborn and King, 2021). Three days after his inauguration, President Trump imposed a hiring freeze on the federal government, like several of his Republican predecessors had done, with the goal of stopping growth in the federal workforce until a comprehensive plan to reduce the size of the federal civil service could be devised and implemented.

Less than two months later, on March 13, 2017, the President issued Executive Order 13781 requiring the Director of the U.S. Office of Management and Budget (OMB) to develop a plan to "reorganize governmental functions and eliminate unnecessary agencies …, components of agencies, and agency programs" (Federal Register, 2017). Later that same week, on March 16, the President submitted a "budget blueprint" to Congress calling for significant reductions in spending. On April 12, 2017, OMB Director Mick Mulvaney issued a detailed memorandum to the heads of executive departments and agencies requiring them to submit plans for reform consistent with the President's budget plan and specifying workforce reductions, the elimination or reorganization of agencies and programs, and proposals for maximizing employee performance (Mulvaney, 2017). Departments and agencies were to submit their proposals in September of 2017.

OMB reviewed departmental and agency plans for reform and used them as the basis for a report issued on June 21, 2018 that specified a plan for comprehensive reform of the federal executive branch (U.S. Office of Management and Budget, 2018). The published plan was produced with numerous color photographs and quotes from ordinary citizens. The document argued that the public was "frustrated with government's ability to deliver its mission in an effective, efficient, and secure way" (U.S. Office of Management and Budget, 2018, p. 4). The authors of the report may have meant to refer to a perception of government's *inability* to deliver on its mission, but the quote is accurate. The plan addressed a wide range of organizations and programs and contained proposals that were dramatic, if not radical. For example, the plan called for the Department of Education and the Department of Labor to be merged into one Cabinet-level agency and argued for the privatization of the U.S. Postal Service. Numerous other agencies or programs were to be consolidated or eliminated. The plan also echoed broad criticisms of the federal personnel system made within conservative circles (see, e.g., Devine, 2017). The document claimed that the existing personnel structure was "archaic" without explaining precisely what the problems were that made it so outdated (U.S. Office of Management and Budget, 2018, p. 51). The argument was made by assertion rather than with evidence, as when the authors of the plan proclaimed that there is "broad acknowledgement" that the personnel system is ineffective, and what is needed is a system designed to "meet 21st Century needs" (U.S. Office of Management and Budget, 2018, p. 51). The plan proposed a dramatic "reorganization" of OPM that if implemented would place authority for personnel policy even more explicitly and directly in the hands of the President than it was when OPM was established in 1979.

Targeting the Office of Personnel Management

Under the plan, all authority for personnel policy formation and oversight would be placed within OMB in the Executive Office of the President

(U.S. Office of Management and Budget, 2018, p. 51). The exercise of this responsibility would be supervised by a director who served at the pleasure of the President and whose appointment did not require Senate approval. This would mean that policy decisions regarding public personnel management would be controlled directly by the White House. Other "operational" functions performed by OPM, including management of the Federal Employees Retirement System, oversight of various health insurance programs, and the delivery of fee-based direct personnel services to federal agencies were all to be housed within the General Services Administration (GSA) (U.S. Office of Management and Budget, 2018, p. 51). The GSA is the agency that maintains and provides supplies for federal buildings. It had no history or expertise in the delivery of human resources management services. Once these reforms were implemented, OPM would no longer exist as a distinct executive branch agency.

In addition to these changes, the National Background Investigations Bureau (NBIB), a division within OPM responsible for background checks on federal employees and applicants, was to be moved to the Department of Defense (DOD) in its entirety. Earlier, in December of 2017, the National Defense Authorization Act (NDAA) for Fiscal Year 2018 required a phased transfer of background investigations for DOD personnel to the Defense Department. This transfer involved 70 percent of the work of the NBIB (U.S. Office of Management and Budget, 2018, p. 115). The inclusion of this provision in the FY 2018 NDAA was accomplished at the urging of the Trump Administration. The reorganization plan published in June of 2018 called for the remaining 30 percent of the government's background investigations also to be transferred to DOD. The transfer of this responsibility out of OPM was a major issue because background investigations had become an important source of OPM's operational revenue. Beginning during the Clinton Administration, appropriations for OPM were reduced dramatically and the agency was required to operate on a fee-for-service basis. That is, OPM would provide direct assistance on the implementation of personnel policies and practices to federal agencies upon their request, and those agencies would pay OPM for the services provided. The loss of authority for background investigations would substantially reduce the revenue flowing to OPM.

The individual at OMB who became the chief advocate of these reforms was Margaret Weichert, who came to government from the private sector finance and information technology industries. Weichert was nominated by President Trump and confirmed as OMB's Deputy Director for Management on February 28, 2018. In addition, Weichert became the Acting Director of OPM on October 5, 2018 while retaining her position at OMB. The previous Director of OPM, Jeff Pon, was nominated by President Trump and confirmed by the Senate in March of 2018, but Trump dismissed him in October of 2018 because he was insufficiently supportive of the Administration's plan to dissolve the agency he was appointed to lead. While Pon did not speak out publicly against the plan, he reportedly told members of Congress that the changes would require legislative revision of Title 5 of the U.S. Code (Yoder and Rein, 2018). Despite the fact that Pon's reported statement was true, it was sufficient reason for the Administration to remove him. Pon served only seven months, from March 9, 2018 to October 5, 2018. Prior to his appointment as OPM Director, Pon was a respected human resources specialist and had served in a senior position at OPM during the George W. Bush Administration. He was the first Senate-confirmed Director for OPM since Katherine Archuleta's resignation in 2015 following a breach of the agency's IT system and the theft of information on 20 million federal employees and retirees.

On March 5, 2019, the Senate Committee on Homeland Security and Governmental Affairs received President Trump's nomination of Dale Cabaniss to be the Director of OPM. Cabaniss had previously served as chair of the Federal Labor Relations Authority under the George W. Bush Administration. She had worked previously also on the Senate Appropriations and Homeland Security and Governmental Affairs committees on issues related to the federal civil service.

While the Cabaniss nomination was under consideration in the Senate, the Trump Administration began an aggressive push for the transfer of OPM operational functions to the GSA. Acting Director Weichert released a document in mid-May outlining the case for the reform and held a "roundtable" meeting with news reporters on May 15, 2019 to discuss the proposal. Weichert cited the 2015 data breach as evidence of OPM's outdated IT system and argued that transfer of OPM's IT functions to the GSA would resolve that problem. Weichert also argued that the Congressionally mandated transfer of the NBIB to the DOD so seriously strained OPM's financial resources that the folding of OPM into the GSA was necessary to secure savings needed to ensure the survival of OPM's functions. This argument by Weichert was disingenuous; however, given that the transfer was initially proposed by the Trump Administration; the inclusion of the transfer of responsibility for background investigations for DOD personnel (70 percent of all investigations) was included in the NDAA for Fiscal Year 2018 at the urging of the Trump Administration; and the transfer of responsibility of the remaining 30 percent of all investigations to DOD was accomplished directly by the Trump Administration. In short, the Trump Administration pushed for and secured the transfer of the NBIB to the DOD, then Trump officials (specifically Weichert) argued that the transfer left OPM financially vulnerable, and hence reorganization in the form of moving OPM operational activities to the GSA was necessary to secure the "financial and operational stability" of OPM's mission (OPM, 2019).

Weichert also argued that the shift of personnel policy authority to OMB would increase "operational excellence" regarding the federal workforce (Chappellet-Lanier, 2019). This advantage would be achieved because officials within OMB could address human resources management issues on a government-wide basis rather than simply developing policy for federal organizations covered by Title 5 of the U.S. Code – which was OPM's mandate. Of course, Title 5 covers almost all of the federal civil service including all employees in in the federal executive branch other than those in the Excepted Service.

Although the President had authority to initiate all of the substantial reforms under consideration, legislation would be necessary (as OPM Director Pon had claimed) to revise provisions of Title 5 specifying the functions of OPM. Those provisions were placed into the law by the Civil Service Reform Act of 1978. The Trump Administration developed a detailed legislative proposal and forwarded it to the Speaker of the U.S. House of Representatives, Representative Nancy Pelosi, and other Democratic and Republican leaders in both the House and Senate on May 16, 2019 (U.S. Office of Management and Budget, 2019). The proposed bill was titled the "Administrative Services Merger Act of 2019." Among other things, the legislation amended Title 5 by striking current language regarding OPM and the Director of OPM and specifying the establishment within the GSA of an "Office of Personnel Management" (U.S. Office of Management and Budget, 2019). That Office was to be headed by a "Director" who would "perform personnel management functions designated by the Administrator of General Services." The legislation would also establish an "Office of Federal Workforce Policy" within OMB. This new organization would "provide overall strategic direction and coordination of workforce policy and regulations for all Executive agencies" and would "aid the President, as the President may request, in preparing Federal workforce policies and otherwise advise the President on actions that may be taken to promote an efficient and effective Federal workforce" (U.S. Office of Management and Budget, 2019). The Office of Federal Workforce Policy was to be led by an "Administrator" appointed by the President without Senate confirmation (U.S. Office of Management and Budget, 2019; Wagner, 2019b). The "Administrator" would report directly to the Deputy Director for Management of the OMB (a position held by Margaret Weichert at the time).

The Hearing in the House of Representatives

Reaction to the proposed personnel reform was decidedly negative among Democrats in Congress and leaders of federal employee unions. Some Republicans also criticized the reform package for a lack of analysis to support the proposal (Wagner, 2020). Five days after the Administration's legislative proposal was announced, on May 21, 2019, the Subcommittee on Government Operations of the U.S. House of Representatives Committee on Oversight and Reform held a hearing on the proposed Bill (U.S. House of Representatives, 2019a).[1] The subcommittee was Chaired by Democratic Representative Gerald E. Connolly of Virginia. The hearing was given the arguably hyperbolic title: "The Administration's War on a Merit-Based Civil Service," and it proceeded in a manner consistent with the sentiment expressed in that title. The key witness was Margaret Weichert, but testimony was also provided by J. David Cox, Sr., the President of the American Federation of Government Employees; Ken Thomas, the President of the National Active and Retired Federal Employees; and Linda M. Springer, a former Director of the Office of Personnel Administration under President George W. Bush. In an opening statement, Chairman Connolly described the Administration's plan as an effort to "eliminate the independence of the civil service" by placing authority for "merit policymaking functions" within the White House where it would be shielded from direct Congressional oversight. Connolly argued that "the Administration's proposal was developed without input from key stakeholders, including Congress, Federal employees, Federal annuitants, and the private sector" and that it was released without any data or evidence to support its goals." Connolly concluded his statement by arguing that "our federal work force is our greatest asset. Improving OPM ought to be a bipartisan goal, but revitalizing OPM requires careful planning and a clear understanding of its problems." Connolly's House of Representatives District was in the northern Virginia suburbs of Washington D.C. and was home, of course, to a large number of federal employees who opposed the Trump reform. When Chairman Connolly described the proposed reform as posing a threat to the "independence of the civil service," that was, from his view, a negative feature of the proposal that was oriented toward increasing the politicization of the federal workforce. Advocates for the reform, of course, saw it differently; they saw it as an effort to reclaim the President's constitutional authority to manage the executive branch of government.

In her testimony at the hearing, Margaret Weichert described the Administration's plan as one intended to "modernize OPM and better support the Federal work force and merit systems principles." She argued that the current personnel system was in "crisis," and that it had failed to "meet modern work force needs." As noted earlier, Weichert pointed to what she considered OPM's inadequate capacity in information technology and asserted that the tasks of OPM "became even harder once Congress transferred the National Background Investigations Bureau to the Department of Defense, moving with it thousands of employees and more than a billion dollars in funding." The Trump Administration's role in facilitating that transfer of authority to the DOD was not mentioned.

For their part, representatives from federal employee unions were strongly opposed to the reorganization. David Cox, President of the American Federation of Government Employees, described the Trump Administration's proposal in strident terms as "reckless, ill-conceived, and potentially dangerous." He began his comments by accurately stating that "The civil service is the most underappreciated pillar of our democracy, and he added, "It is far more fragile than many people realize." Cox argued that the GSA did not have the experience or expertise to manage human resources programs. The GSA "administers contracts and leases office space and fleets of vehicles," he noted. Cox also argued that the transfer of personnel policy responsibility to the White House would inappropriately politicize federal human resources management.

Ken Thomas, the President of the National Active and Retired Federal Employees, agreed with the assessment offered by Cox. Thomas continued by observing that the central mission of OPM is to manage the federal workforce to ensure competence and political neutrality. If the proposed reforms were put into place, there would be fewer protections in place to guard against "politically motivated personnel decisions." Linda Springer, the Director of OPM from June of 2005 to August of 2008, also spoke out against the reform. Springer suggested that the reform proposal was "the culmination of years of intent by OMB, spanning administrations of both parties, to acquire ownership of personnel management from OPM." Springer argued that there had been insufficient analysis of the implications of the reform, that personnel services would not fit well organizationally into the GSA, and that placing responsibility for human resources policy in OMB (which is in the Executive Office of the President) risked placing responsibility for federal personnel "right back into the place where the spoils and patronage system had taken hold" prior to passage of the Pendleton Act.

The points raised by Director Springer warrant careful consideration. The creation of OPM by President Carter was accomplished as a means of enhancing presidential authority, or to state it differently, it provided a structure that would allow a fuller and more direct exercise of the President's constitutional authority. One could argue that obstacles to the proper exercise of presidential authority were minimized by the Carter reforms. The effort to diminish OPM by moving its policy-making functions to OMB within the Executive Office of the President did have the appearance of a "turf" war between administrative units. The reform effort was led by OMB, and clearly, that organization would have its authority substantially increased if the reform were successful. OMB was, since its inception, primarily a budget agency. The proposed transfer of personnel policy authority to the agency would significantly increase the agency's responsibility for federal management and would presumably give substantive meaning to the "M" in OMB.

In the weeks following the House of Representatives hearing on the Administration's proposal, and in the face of opposition from members of Congress and employee unions, OPM took no action to produce documents and analyses, including cost-benefit analyses of the reform the House Sub-Committee had requested. Dale Cabaniss was eventually confirmed by the Senate on September 11, 2019 to serve as OPM Director. Cabaniss assumed that position on September 16, and Margaret Weichert stepped down as Acting Director to return exclusively to her responsibilities as Deputy Director for Management at OMB, although, notably, she continued to advocate for the personnel reform from her position at OMB.

The NAPA Study

On December 20, 2019, the NDAA for Fiscal Year 2020 was passed into law (U.S. Congress, 2019). The law contained a provision (Section 1112) stating, in part, that "No person may assign, transfer, transition, merge, or consolidate any function, responsibility, authority, service, system, or program that is assigned in law to the Office of Personnel Management to or with the General Services Administration, the Office of Management and Budget, or the Executive Office of the President" until at least 180 days after the completion of an independent study of OPM's responsibilities by the National Academy of Public Administration. This provision of the FY 2020 NDAA effectively called a halt to efforts to implement the OPM reforms. A panel of NAPA Fellows was assembled to conduct the study and work was underway in the spring of 2020.[2] The completed NAPA report was submitted to Congress and OPM in March of 2021. By this time, the Biden Administration was in office. The NAPA report recommended against the types of reforms proposed for OPM under President Trump. Instead, the report concluded that Congress should:

> clarify and redefine the role and mission of OPM as the federal government's enterprise-wide, independent human capital agency and steward of the merit system for all civilian personnel systems and employees, responsible for providing government-wide leadership in strategic human capital management.
> *National Academy of Public Administration (2021, p. 3)*

Overall, the NAPA panel made 23 specific recommendations including increases in funding to OPM for the provision of technical services on a "no-fee" basis to federal agencies and to significantly modernize OPM's IT infrastructure.

While the NAPA study was underway, however, members of the Trump Administration continued to work to implement the reform despite the Congressional ban on doing so. Indeed, one report indicated that OPM "transferred the staff for the Chief Human Capital Officers Council to the GSA and was accused on multiple occasions of trying to subvert the ban on implementation" of the reforms (Wagner, 2020). Nevertheless, the Trump administration eventually capitulated and four months prior to the publication of the NAPA report, in late October of 2020, the Administration officially abandoned the OPM reform effort (Wagner, 2020).

The OPM Proposal in Retrospect

Two additional points regarding OMB and OPM under President Trump deserve mention. Margaret Weichert left her position as Deputy Director for Management at OMB to return to the private sector on March 25, 2020. Her departure meant that the Administration's major voice for the reform was gone. In addition, Dale Cabaniss abruptly left her position as Director of OPM on March 17, 2020 after only six months on the job. Reports were that she objected to taking direction from John McEntee, a 29-year-old former campaign aid whom Trump had named the Director of the White House Personnel Office (the office responsible for assisting in filling political appointments), and Paul Dans, an attorney with no experience in federal personnel policy, who was appointed to be a White House liaison and advisor to the Director of OPM (Lippman, 2020). Representative Gerry Connolly said in a statement: "If these reports [regarding the reasons for Cabaniss' departure] are true, then the Trump administration's mismanagement and political appointees have once again brought chaos to the federal workforce" (Samuels and Budryk, 2020, see also, Rein, 2020). As this story illustrates, there was significant

TABLE 5.1 OPM Directors under President Trump

1.	Kathleen McGettigan	Acting; January 19, 2017 to March 9, 2018
2.	Jeff Tien Han Pon	March 9, 2018 to October 5, 2018
3.	Margaret Weichert	Acting; October 5, 2018 to September 16, 2019
4.	Dale Cabaniss	September 16, 2019 to March 17, 2020
5.	Michael Rigas	Acting; March 18, 2020 to January 20, 2021

instability at OPM during the Trump years. Table 5.1 provides a list of individuals who served as Director of OPM under President Trump.

The tasks performed by OPM include the formulation and implementation of federal policy regarding employee recruitment, examination, selection, training, compensation, and discipline. These are essential functions for effective government. Because the work of the government is dependent upon the labor of qualified employees, these activities are of critical importance. OPM is described as an "independent" executive agency, but it is independent only in the sense that it is not a subunit of some other larger organization. Title II of the Civil Service Reform Act of 1978 states that "The Office of Personnel Management is an independent establishment in the executive branch" (U.S. Congress, Public Law 95-454, 92 Stat. 1119). However, OPM is led by a Director who serves and is answerable to the President. This structure provides accountability for federal personnel policy to the American people through the President.

There are still calls from some conservatives for OPM to be abolished and for its functions to be contracted out to private firms or shifted to other federal organizations such as OMB (see, e.g., Moran, 2024). An alternative option would be to keep the present structure and the accountability it provides but bolster the agency by giving it the resources it needs to function as it should. This means that Congress should appropriate money necessary for OPM to thoroughly update its information technology infrastructure and to permit the agency to escape the funding impediment imposed by the fact that it operates largely on a fee-for-service basis. Implementation of the recommendations made in the 2021 NAPA report would constitute movement in that direction (National Academy of Public Administration, 2021).

Notes

1 All quotations in the following paragraphs are taken from the transcript of the hearing. See U.S. House of Representatives (2019a).
2 The author of this book was a member of the NAPA panel assembled to produce the report.

6

THE CREATION OF SCHEDULE F

On October 21, 2020, less than two weeks before the November presidential election, President Trump issued a new Executive Order that presented his most direct challenge to the federal merit system's competitive service. This was Executive Order 13957, entitled "Creating Schedule F in the Excepted Service" (*Federal Register*, Vol. 85, No. 207, 2020, pp. 67631–67635). The Order required all agency heads to transfer all positions within their organizations that have a "confidential, policy-determining, policy-making, or policy-advocating character" into a new employment category in the Excepted Service designated "Schedule F." Despite a longstanding norm of not requiring employees to move involuntarily from the Competitive Service to the Excepted Service, employees in those positions identified for transfer were expected to move when their positions were moved. If they wished to avoid assignment in the Excepted Service, they could presumably seek transfer to other jobs in the Competitive Service or resign. This expectation was the same as the Administration's earlier expectation regarding the transfer of Administrative Law Judges to the newly established Schedule E within the Excepted Service.

The Organization of the Federal Service

A full appreciation of the scope of change imposed by Executive Order 13957 requires some familiarity with the basic structure of the federal civil service and the broad classes into which individuals are hired. Currently, there are approximately 2.1 million non-postal service federal civilian employees.[1]

DOI: 10.4324/9781032656380-6

These federal civilian employees are, for the most part, distributed into the "Competitive Service," the "Excepted Service," and the "Senior Executive Service."[2]

The *Competitive Service* contains approximately 70 percent of the non-postal federal civilian workforce (U.S. Office of Personnel Management, 2018). Workers in the Competitive Service are career employees who receive their jobs through open and competitive examination processes designed to measure qualifications. The *Excepted Service* includes positions in the non-postal federal service "excepted" from the standard competitive examination hiring system. Qualifications are still assessed, but for various reasons, usual examination procedures are not used or the exams utilized are not competitive. Nearly 30 percent of the federal service consists of employees in the Excepted Service.

Prior to the issuance of Executive Order 13957, there were five distinct employment schedules in the Excepted Service, as outlined in Table 6.1. Schedules A and B were established early in the history of the civil service. Schedule A is for positions for which examinations are not "practicable." Specific positions for attorneys or chaplains, or positions for which there is a critical need, are cited as examples. Schedule A is also used today to hire persons with disabilities. Schedule B includes positions for which *competitive* examinations are not practicable, but non-competitive examinations that measure minimum qualification standards are used. Schedule C, established in 1953 by President Eisenhower, is reserved for lower-level political positions. Schedule D was established by President Obama to facilitate the employment of students in the Presidential Management Fellows Program and to fill positions involving science, technology, engineering, or mathematics (STEM) occupations. Finally, President Trump established Schedule E to exempt Administrative Law Judges from competitive selection procedures, as noted earlier in Chapter 4, *supra*. In addition, Trump's Order establishing Schedule E removed employees in Schedules A, C, D, and E from civil service rules providing guarantees of due process and fairness in termination procedures. The President had constitutional authority to make this change, and it resulted in a significant shift in the personnel rules covering these employees.

The third major category of employment in the federal service, the *Senior Executive Service* (SES), was established through the Civil Service Reform Act of 1978 and consists of approximately 8,000 top-level federal managers. Ninety percent of the government-wide positions in the SES are career employees selected competitively. However, up to ten percent may be noncareer political appointees who are not part of the competitive service. Career SES members must serve a one-year probationary period.

TABLE 6.1 Employment Schedules in the Excepted Service Prior to Executive Order 13957

Schedule A (Established in 1903[a])	Positions that are "not of a confidential or policy-determining nature for which it is not practicable to examine applicants." Schedule A is used today in the employment of persons with documented disabilities, persons who fulfill a critical need, and for other similar purposes.
Schedule B (Established in 1910[b])	Positions that are "not of a confidential or policy-determining nature" that are filled through noncompetitive examinations.
Schedule C (Established March 31, 1953 by Executive Order 10440)	Positions that are "policy-determining or involve a close and confidential working relationship with the head of an agency or other key appointed officials." These employees are "political appointees below the cabinet or subcabinet levels."
Schedule D (Established December 27, 2010 by Executive Order 13562)	Positions that are "not of a confidential or policy-determining character for which competitive examination makes it difficult to recruit a sufficient number of certain students or recent graduates. Examples of schedule D positions include those involving science, technology, engineering, or mathematics (STEM) occupations and positions in the Presidential Management Fellows Program."
Schedule E (Established July 10, 2018, by Executive Order 13843)	Schedule E is used for the employment of Administrative Law Judges. Executive Order 13843 also exempted all positions in Schedules A, C, D, and E from civil service rules governing removals.

Source: Information on Schedules A through D is from Shimabukuro and Staman (2019) and from the U.S. Office of Personnel Management (2018). Information on Schedule E is from Executive Order 13843 of 2018.

[a] The Pendleton Act of 1883 provided that positions identified by the President or the U.S. Civil Service Commission would be excepted from the requirement that selection be based on competitive examination. The term "Schedule A" was first used in a report of the Civil Service Commission in 1904 to refer to those positions. See U.S. Civil Service Commission (1904).

[b] Positions filled through noncompetitive examinations were separated from Schedule A and placed into a new Schedule B in 1910. See Van Riper (1958, p. 207).

Procedural Due Process Requirement in Terminations

All employees in the Competitive Service, those in the SES who are not in political positions, and employees in Schedule B of the Excepted Service are promised that dismissal or removal from employment will be only for cause once they have successfully passed through a preliminary probationary (or trial) period. The probationary period is the period of initial employment, typically the first year on the job, during which an employee may be dismissed without cause stated, although dismissal obviously cannot be based on an illegal reason such as race, ethnicity, sex, age, or political party affiliation. The probationary period is when a new employee demonstrates their ability and suitability for their position, and the employing agency may remove employees with no reason given. However, once the employee passes successfully through the probationary period, the promise is made that removal in the future will only be for justifiable reasons associated with poor performance.

This promise that removal will be only for just cause rests primarily on presidential prerogative but has become a hallmark of traditional civil service merit systems over many decades. It is intended to prevent the removal of employees for political or otherwise unwarranted reasons.[3] In the absence of any just cause for removal, employees given this promise have a reasonable basis for expecting their employment to continue. This reasonable expectation means, in turn, that covered employees have what the U.S. Supreme Court has labeled a "property interest" in their jobs. Because the U.S. Constitution prohibits the government from denying persons "life, liberty, or property" without due process of law, any employee with a property interest in his/her job must be provided procedural due process.[4] This means that they must be given notice prior to removal and given an opportunity to respond to allegations against them, including through a hearing.

The U.S. Supreme Court set out procedural due process requirements in the dismissal of public employees in 1985 in *Cleveland Board of Education* v. *Loudermill* (470 U.S. 532). The Court's decision in this instance actually addressed two separate cases that arose from the Cleveland, Ohio, area and were consolidated on appeal by the Sixth Circuit Court of Appeals in Cincinnati, Ohio.

The first of these cases involved Mr. James Loudermill, who was hired as a security guard by the Cleveland, Ohio, Board of Education in 1979. When completing the employment application, Mr. Loudermill answered "no" to a question asking whether he had ever been convicted of a felony. Mr. Loudermill signed the application attesting that, to the best of his knowledge, all information on the form was true. Eleven months later, during a routine examination of employee records, the School Board discovered that Loudermill had been convicted of a felony (larceny) years earlier in 1968. The Board moved to dismiss him immediately for dishonesty on the employment application. Mr. Loudermill was given no opportunity prior to his termination to respond to the charge of dishonesty or to challenge his dismissal. His termination was effective as of November 13, 1980.

After his dismissal, Mr. Loudermill filed an appeal with the Cleveland Civil Service Commission. A referee was appointed by the Commission to review the case. At a January 29, 1981 hearing, Loudermill argued that he had thought that his 1968 larceny conviction was for a misdemeanor rather than a felony. The referee recommended reinstatement, but in July of 1981, the Commission announced it would uphold the dismissal. Mr. Loudermill then filed suit in the Federal District Court for the Northern District of Ohio. The District Court dismissed the case and argued that the School Board had followed proper procedure. Loudermill then appealed to the Sixth Circuit.

The second case involved Mr. Richard Donnelly, a bus mechanic for the Parma, Ohio, Board of Education. The City of Parma is a suburb of Cleveland. Mr. Donnelly was fired in August 1977 for failing an eye examination. Like Loudermill, Donnelly was given no prior notice or opportunity to challenge the dismissal before it was effective. Donnelly appealed to the Parma Civil Service Commission after his termination. A year later, after the Commission heard his appeal, the Commission ordered that Donnelly be reinstated, but he was not to receive back pay. Mr. Donnelly then filed suit in the Federal District Court for the Northern District of Ohio, but in an action similar to that in the Loudermill case, the District Court dismissed the case. Donnelly then appealed to the Sixth Circuit.

The Court of Appeals for the Sixth Circuit consolidated the Loudermill and Donnelly cases. After hearing arguments, the Circuit Court ruled that Mr. Loudermill and Mr. Donnelly had been deprived of their due process rights by their government employers. The Court reasoned that both petitioners were entitled to notice and a chance to respond before their terminations took effect. The local school boards appealed to the U.S. Supreme Court.

In considering these cases, the Supreme Court first determined that the State of Ohio statute governing local civil service employees created a property interest in employment for Loudermill and Donnelly by mandating that dismissal would be for just cause only. Under those circumstances, employees have a reasonable expectation to retain their positions provided no just cause for their termination is present. Once the government creates the property interest in this manner, the Constitution's due-process clause is triggered, which prohibits the government from denying a person their "property" without procedural due process. The Court reasoned that procedural due process must, at a minimum, include prior notice and a right to respond to allegations of wrongdoing, including through a hearing, before termination is carried out. As a practical matter, then, the process of dismissal is slowed down. While the Loudermill and Donnelly cases involved employees of local school boards, the principles articulated by the Supreme Court apply to public employee dismissal procedures at all levels of government.

The constraint on removal and other forms of adverse action, imposed by due process requirements, helps form the basis for civil service rules and employee protections that give rise to conservative derision and contempt. Certainly, dismissal of employees with these rights is more difficult than it would otherwise be if those rights did not exist, but removal is not impossible (see, Kettl, 2020a). In a report published in 2015, the Merit Systems Protection Board indicated that "From FY 2000-2014, over 77,000 full-time, permanent, Federal employees were discharged as a result of performance and/or conduct issues" (U.S. Merit Systems Protection Board, 2015, p. 41). That number, however, reflects actions over 15 years. In that context, it is not very large. All employees in the Excepted Service were also given the promise that termination would be for just cause only until President Trump's Executive Order creating Schedule E removed that promise from workers in Schedules A, C, D, and E, as noted earlier, and as a result, employees in those schedules lost the due process rights in termination proceedings they had enjoyed earlier.

The Goals of Schedule F

In general, the purpose of Schedule F was to achieve two goals: (1) *appointment flexibility* and (2) *removal flexibility* for positions that are "not normally subject to change as a result of a Presidential transition" but are nevertheless of a "confidential, policy-determining, policy-making, or policy-advocating character." *Appointment flexibility* was achieved by excepting the process of filling these positions from the rules mandating that the selection of employees will be based on the results of open and competitive examinations designed to measure applicant qualifications, as is required in the competitive service. According to the Order, this provision would give agency heads the "additional flexibility to assess prospective appointees without the limitations imposed by competitive service selection procedures" (*Federal Register*, Vol. 85, No. 207, 2020, p. 67631). As noted previously, incumbent employees were expected to move with their positions, but in the case of future vacancies, hiring rules would be flexible and non-competitive. Precisely how selection would be made in those instances, however, was not specified. Agency heads were, in effect, given largely unfettered discretion to hire whomever they wanted for positions they determined were of a "confidential, policy-determining, policy-making, or policy-advocating character." As the Order stated, "agencies should be able to assess candidates without proceeding through complicated and elaborate competitive service processes or rating procedures that do not necessarily reflect their particular needs" (*Federal Register*, Vol. 85, No. 207, 2020, p. 67632). Presumably, positions in Schedule F would be filled in a manner similar to that used to select political appointees.

Removal flexibility was achieved by exempting positions in Schedule F from "the adverse action procedures set forth in Chapter 75 of Title 5 of the United States Code" (*Federal Register*, Vol. 85, No. 207, 2020, p. 67632). Those procedures are present to ensure fairness in the discharge or termination of employees in the competitive service. Among other things, competitive service employees must be given due process in procedures associated with termination as set out by the Supreme Court in the *Loudermill* case. These procedures include prior notice of pending termination and a right to respond to allegations brought against them before they are removed from service. Because Schedule F employees were exempt from this protection, relative security of tenure, which is a hallmark of traditional civil service, was eliminated for them. Employees moved to Schedule F would become modified "at will" workers. However, prohibited personnel practices, including discriminating against an employee or applicant based on race, color, religion, sex, national origin, age, disability, marital status, or political affiliation, were maintained for Schedule F workers. Removal procedures for Schedule F employees were streamlined by eliminating due process requirements, but the government did not have a completely free hand in dismissing those workers.

Another critical aspect of the Schedule F Executive Order was a provision that required agency heads to request the Federal Labor Relations Authority to determine whether Schedule F employees could remain in collective bargaining units given their responsibilities for formulating, determining, or influencing public policy (*Federal Register*, Vol. 85, No. 207, 2020, p. 67634). One could presume that an unstated assumption of proponents for Schedule F was that employees within that schedule would lose union affiliation and collective bargaining rights. Of course, if those employees were no longer subject to union representation, they would also lose the ability to grieve specific adverse personnel actions, including terminations, as discussed in Chapter 4, *supra*.

Executive Order 13957, the Schedule F order, was designed to move large numbers of employees from the Competitive Service and place them into a new category in the Excepted Service (Schedule F) where selection would be flexible and noncompetitive and dismissal procedures would be unencumbered by procedural due process requirements (Wagner, 2020; Lipton, 2020). The Order began with the following statement:

"To effectively carry out the broad array of activities assigned to the executive branch under law, the President and his appointees must rely on men and women in the Federal service employed in positions of a confidential, policy-determining, policy-making, or policy-advocating character. Faithful execution of the law requires that the President have appropriate management oversight regarding this select cadre of professionals."

Federal Register (Vol. 85, No. 207, 2020, p. 67631)

The Executive Order cites the 2016 Merit Systems Survey of federal employees, which found that less than 25 percent of federal workers believe their agencies deal effectively with poor performers. The Executive Order also states:

"agencies should have a greater degree of appointment flexibility with respect to these employees than is afforded by the existing competitive service process,

and ...

conditions of good administration make necessary an exception to the competitive hiring rules and examinations for career positions in the Federal service of a confidential, policy-determining, policy-making, or policy-advocating character."

Federal Register (Vol. 85, No. 207, 2020, p. 67631)

"Conditions of good Administration similarly make necessary excepting such positions from the adverse action procedures set forth in chapter 75 of title 5, United States Code. Chapter 75 of Title 5, United States Code, requires agencies to comply with extensive procedures before taking adverse action against an employee."

Federal Register (Vol. 85, No. 207, 2020, p. 67632)

The changes initiated by Executive Order 13957 would have brought tens of thousands of federal workers (or more) into Schedule F and would have fundamentally altered core principles of merit that have structured federal employment since the end of the Nineteenth Century. Trump's Order was an attempt to reassert Presidential authority over the executive branch of government by better controlling the federal civilian workforce. In late November of 2020, after the Presidential election was called for President Biden, the U.S. Office of Management and Budget rushed to shift 68 percent of its workforce into Schedule F, and other agencies also prepared lists of employees to be transferred (U.S. Government Accountability Office, 2022).

President Trump's Executive Order creating Schedule F was a remarkable demonstration of how long-held principles and structures regarding the federal service can be upended simply through the exercise of Presidential prerogative (Moynihan, 2021). There was an immediate backlash against the Order, with many civic leaders, academics, and professional associations connected to public Administration expressing concern about the erosion of merit principles and damage done to important values such as neutral competence and due process.[5] On January 22, 2021 (two days after his inauguration), President Biden, through Executive Order 14003, rescinded Trump's Order creating Schedule F, along with the three earlier orders from May 25, 2018, that made it easier to fire federal employees, regulated the practice of collective bargaining, and restricted federal employees in official union positions from conducting union business while at work. In his Order rescinding Trump's policies, President Biden declared, "Career civil servants are the backbone of the Federal workforce, providing the expertise and experience necessary for the critical functioning of the Federal Government. It is the policy of the United States to protect, empower, and rebuild the career Federal workforce" (see Executive Order 14033 of January 22, 2021). Despite this, former members of the Trump Administration are committed to a reinstatement of Schedule F should Trump or any other Republican regain the White House in 2024 or later.

The OPM Regulation Prohibiting a New Schedule F

In response to the possibility of a future Republican Administration reinstituting Schedule F, the Biden Administration began work to formulate and issue a regulation to prohibit such action. The final version of this rule, issued by OPM, was published on April 9, 2024, in the *Federal Register* (Vol. 89, No. 69, p. 24982) and was scheduled to become effective on May 9, 2024. As stated in the final version of the regulation, the purpose is to:

> reinforce and clarify longstanding civil service protections and merit system principles, codified in law, as they relate to the involuntary movement of Federal employees and positions from the competitive service to the excepted service, or from one excepted service schedule to another.
>
> *Federal Register (Vol. 89, No. 69, p. 24982)*

The new regulation noted that career civil servants have "institutional experience, subject matter expertise, and technical knowledge" necessary to assess policy options and implementation strategies effectively (*Federal Register*, Vol. 89, No. 69, p. 24982). They know what has worked in the past and what efforts have failed. They know the advantages and disadvantages of different policy options. This expertise and institutional memory are valuable for the government generally and for political appointees who oversee career employees. The regulation also notes that "a mere difference of opinion with leadership does not qualify as misconduct or unacceptable performance ... that would warrant an adverse action" against a career civil servant (*Federal Register*, Vol. 89, No. 69, p. 24982). The rule further states that the ability of career civil servants to:

> offer their objective analyses and educated views when carrying out their duties, without fear of reprisal or loss of employment, contributes to the reasoned consideration of policy options.
>
> *Federal Register (Vol. 89, No. 69, p. 24982)*

The final OPM rule also specifies that:

> civil servants in the competitive service or excepted service who ... have fulfilled their probationary or trial period requirement ... will retain the rights previously accrued upon an involuntary move from the competitive service to the excepted service, or from one excepted service schedule to another.
>
> *Federal Register (Vol. 89, No. 69, p. 24983)*

The rule also interpreted the phrases "confidential, policy-determining, policy-making, or policy-advocating" or "confidential or policy-determining" as applying specifically within the law to positions filled by noncareer political appointees (Federal Register, Vol. 89, No. 69, p. 24983). By specifying a precise legal meaning of these phrases, the rule eschews their use or application in any more common manner as was done in President Trump's Schedule F order.

Will the new OPM regulation prohibit a return of Schedule F under a new Republican Administration? No, that is not likely, but it will make the re-establishment of Schedule F or some similar structure more challenging to implement. Any future presidential administration seeking to reimplement Schedule F must abolish OPM's regulation first. That is possible, but the processes for doing so are cumbersome. A regulation cannot be revoked simply with the stroke of a pen, as can be done with executive orders. Three approaches to regulatory revocation or revision are available. First, the OPM regulation could be challenged in Court.

That strategy is likely to be implemented after the new OPM rule becomes effective. Litigation will take time, however, and success is not guaranteed. Second, a new Republican presidential administration could work with Congress to pass legislation to revise or abolish the regulation. That process will require a Republican majority in the House of Representatives and a filibuster-proof Republican majority in the Senate. Third, a revised regulation could be proposed by new leadership of OPM, subjected to the regular public notice and comment procedures associated with rulemaking under the Administrative Procedures Act of 1946, and then finalized. However, this process could take several months to complete. A legal record justifying the change would be required, and OPM would need to gather and respond to public comments. Only then could a new regulation be issued. However, an interim final rule could be announced more expeditiously. As a result, the new OPM regulation prohibiting the creation of a new employment category in the Excepted Service, similar to President Trump's Schedule F, will operate to delay any reimplementation of that concept but will not stop it. A new version of Schedule F may still be established.

Notes

1 The U.S. Postal Service, which employs approximately six hundred thousand individuals, is considered to be separate from the remainder of the federal service since it is an independent organization managed by a Board of Governors consisting of nine individuals appointed by the President with Senate approval and a Postmaster General and Deputy Postmaster General selected by the Governors.

2 There are other specialized categories of employment as well, such as the U.S. Foreign Service, which provides a distinct personnel system for about 13,000 employees constituting the U.S. Diplomatic Corps. In addition, the "Executive Schedule" is at the top of the federal service and consists of political appointees, including Cabinet members, top departmental officials, and agency directors. There are five pay rates within the Executive Schedule.

3 As noted earlier, this concept is grounded in the Pendleton Act but dates explicitly from President McKinley's Executive Order 101 and President Theodore Roosevelt's Executive Order 371. The concept is also reflected in the Lloyd-LaFollette Act of 1912 concerning the federal classified (i.e., competitive) service.

4 The due process clause is found in the 5th Amendment, which limits the federal government's power, and in the 14th Amendment, limiting the power of states and their local governments. The Constitution prohibits the government from denying a person "life, liberty, or property, without due process of law." As we have noted, a property interest is established when employees are promised that dismissal will be for just cause only, and a reasonable expectation of continued employment is established for the employee, provided there is no just cause for their removal. Importantly,

however, all employees, even probationary employees, have a liberty interest. They may only be terminated in a way that limits their liberty to find new employment if procedural due process is provided. A removal that infringes on an employee's liberty would occur when the removal causes unflattering or harmful information to become known about the employee, thus limiting future employment prospects. As a result, if they are removed, probationary employees are typically not given a reason for the dismissal. Employees who successfully pass through probation are promised that any future removal will be for just cause only and provided procedural due process in termination proceedings.

5 See, for example, the statement by the American Society for Public Administration at https://www.aspanet.org/ASPA/About-ASPA/In-the-Community/Releases/NC-ScheduleF-EO-Repeal.aspx. The Maxwell School of Citizenship and Public Service at Syracuse University, one of the Nation's leading Schools of Public Administration and Policy, issued a similar statement found at: https://www.maxwell.syr.edu/deans/dean_s_announcements/executive_order_13957_puts_the_integrity_of_public_service_at_stake/?utm_source=alumni-announcement&utm_medium=email&utm_campaign=statement-about-executive-order-on-immigration. A wide range of government management experts also expressed concern in the publication *Government Executive*: https://www.govexec.com/management/2020/10/governance-experts-assail-white-house-effort-strip-federal-employees-rights/169499/. See in particular, the *Government Executive* article by Donald F. Kettl (2020b): https://www.govexec.com/management/2020/10/trumps-order-sets-stage-loyalty-tests-thousands-feds/169492/. For a classic statement on the value of politically neutral competence, see Kaufman (1956).

7

CHANGING COURSE AT THE FLRA

Up to this point, we have reviewed the disabling of the Merit Systems Protection Board during the Trump Presidency, Trump's Executive Orders intended to weaken public employee unions and make it easier to fire federal employees, the effort to abolish the Office of Personnel Management and shift the formation of personnel policy into the Office of Management and Budget within the Executive Office of the President, and the establishment of Schedule F as a new category of employment within the Excepted Service in the waning days of the Trump Administration. These actions represent efforts to increase the extent to which federal employees and their associations are subordinate to presidential authority. While these endeavors were largely reversed by the Biden Administration and thus had little lasting impact, they nevertheless point the way for future presidents inclined to achieve an increased level of dominance over the federal executive bureaucracy. However, the story of the Trump presidency's effort to assert control is not complete with the narrative told thus far. Another story remains: the tale of the Federal Labor Relations Authority (FLRA) during the Trump era.

The Role of the FLRA

The FLRA was established by President Carter through his Reorganization Plan No. 2 of 1978 and was included as part of Title VII of the Civil Service Reform Act of 1978 (CSRA), which as we have noted amended Title 5 of the U.S. Code. President Carter wished to see federal sector labor–management relations

DOI: 10.4324/9781032656380-7

moved to a basis in statutory law, and that was accomplished through the CSRA. As we have seen, Title VII of the CSRA is known as the Federal Service Labor–Management Relations Statute (FSLMRS).

Prior to passage of the FSLMRS, collective bargaining in the federal civil service rested exclusively on presidential executive orders. The first authorization came with Executive Order 10988, issued by President Kennedy on January 17, 1962 (*Federal Register*, Vol. 27, No. 13, 1962, pp. 551-556). Kennedy's Order gave federal employees the right to organize through unions and to bargain collectively on specified working conditions consisting largely of personnel policies and their implementation. There was no negotiation over wages or benefits and no right to strike, a position consistent with the Taft/Hartley Act of 1947 that governed private-sector labor relations but contained a specific provision prohibiting federal employees from striking. In addition, neither party was obligated to bargain in good faith under Kennedy's Executive Order. As a result, because employees had no right to strike, management had no real incentive to work for an agreement. When negotiations failed and an impasse was reached, management could continue to move forward with status quo arrangements that had previously existed. Kennedy provided for no formal impasse resolution procedures.

President Nixon addressed these shortcomings in Executive Order 11491, issued on October 29, 1969 (*Federal Register*, Vol. 34, No. 210, 1969, pp. 17605-17615). Nixon's Order required that labor and management bargain in good faith over personnel policy issues subject to negotiations. The Order also established the Federal Services Impasses Panel (FSIP) to assist in resolving impasses by providing for third-party dispute resolution mechanisms, including mediation, fact-finding, and arbitration. Mediation occurs when labor and management bring a neutral third party into the negotiations to help facilitate agreement. The mediator will typically meet separately with labor and management representatives to explore their positions and identify areas where they may be willing to compromise. The mediator will then bring the parties together to discuss the basis for their disagreement and probe ways to resolve their dispute. If mediation fails, which it may do, the next technique used is fact-finding. In this procedure, a neutral third party examines labor and management positions to determine the facts of the case, as a court would do in a judicial context. However, the fact finder cannot impose a decision. The role of the fact finder is merely to recommend decisions based on the observed facts. Finally, when all else fails, the last option is arbitration. In this alternative, the neutral third party hears the views of each party and then formulates a binding resolution. Nixon's Order also established the Federal Labor Relations Council (FLRC) to provide administrative oversight of federal labor relations processes, including bargaining unit determination and union recognition, and to rule on allegations of unfair labor practices. The FLRC was the precursor to today's FLRA. Nixon maintained the prohibition on bargaining over wages and benefits and continued the prohibition on the right to strike.

The framework put in place by President Nixon constituted a reasonably well-functioning system for federal service labor–management relations. Nevertheless, President Ford adjusted Nixon's policies through Executive Order 11838 of February 6, 1975. Ford's Order required that negotiated contracts provide for formal grievance procedures through which disputes over the implementation of contract provisions could be resolved. In addition, Ford specified further restrictions on bargaining by prohibiting negotiations over:

> "matters with respect to the mission of an agency; its budget; its organization; the number of employees; and the numbers, types, and grades of positions or employees assigned to an organizational unit, work project or tour of duty; the technology of performing its work; or its internal security practices."
> *Federal Register, Vol. 40, No. 27, 1975, p. 5745*

President Carter's Reorganization Plan No. 2 of 1978 (effective January 1, 1979, pursuant to Executive Order 12107 of December 28, 1978) replaced Nixon's FLRC with the FLRA, which operates to this day (see Chapter 3, *supra*). However, because the law regarding the federal civil service is specified in Title 5 of the U.S. Code, and because any subsequent President could rescind the executive orders issued by Kennedy, Nixon, Ford, or Carter, President Carter included federal labor–management relations policy as established by his Order and earlier Presidential Executive Orders in the CSRA of 1978 (5 U.S.C. 7101–7135). Thus, Title VII of the CSRA was created, and the resulting FSLMRS was established. The Act amended Title 5 of the U.S. Code to reflect the changes implemented by President Carter's Reorganization Plan and, as a result, placed federal labor–management relations on a statutory footing, making collective bargaining secure from revocation by any future President simply by issuing a new Executive Order.[1]

The FLRA provides administrative oversight and guidance for federal labor–management relations policy, just as Nixon's old FLRC had done. In general, the agency exists to protect federal employee union organizing and bargaining rights. As indicated on the FLRA website, the agency's mission is:

"Protecting rights and facilitating stable relationships among federal agencies, labor organizations, and employees while advancing an effective and efficient government through the administration of the Federal Service Labor-Management Relations Statute."

https://www.flra.gov/about/mission

In pursuing this mission, the FLRA is responsible for defining the boundaries of collective bargaining units and supervising the voting process through which employees in specified units select a union as their exclusive bargaining agent. The agency also rules on questions regarding the negotiability of issues that may arise. Perhaps most importantly, the FLRA is expected to serve as an unbiased adjudicator of appeals from unions and federal agencies of perceived unfair labor practices. The FLRA makes an annual report to the President and Congress on the cases it has heard and the decisions it has made. The authority of the FLRA extends to virtually all non-postal employees in the federal civil service.[2]

The agency consists of three members appointed to five-year terms by the President with the advice and consent of the Senate. As is the case with the MSPB, no more than two members of the FLRA may be from the same political party. In addition, the President designates one member to serve as Chairman of the FLRA.[3] The Chairman is the chief executive and administrative officer of the Authority. The President may remove members of the FLRA only for just cause, including "inefficiency, neglect of duty, or malfeasance in office" (5 U.S. Code, Section 7104). Any member of the FLRA chosen to fill a vacancy will be appointed only for the remainder of the term of the member being replaced.

A General Counsel serving under the FLRA is also appointed by the President with the advice and consent of the Senate for a five-year term. The General Counsel is responsible for investigating complaints of unfair labor practices that the unions or federal agencies lodge. Following the investigation of complaints, the General Counsel will bring complaints that have merit to the FLRA members for resolution. Notably, the FLRA can only consider complaints of unfair labor practices that have been investigated by the General Counsel and recommended to the members of the FLRA for a ruling. The President may remove the General Counsel at any time.

As noted above, another essential subunit of the FLRA is the FSIP. The FSIP was established by President Nixon's Executive Order 11491 of 1969. The agency exists to resolve disputes that occur when collective bargaining negotiations become deadlocked or reach an impasse. Title 5 of the U.S. Code specifies that the FSIP is to be composed of:

> "a Chairman and at least six other members, who shall be appointed by the President, solely on the basis of fitness to perform the duties and functions involved, from among individuals who are familiar with Government operations and knowledgeable in labor-management relations."
>
> *Title 5 U.S.C. subsection 7119*

Currently, there are ten members of the FSIP. All members serve on a part-time basis. Presidential appointments to the Panel are made without Senate confirmation, and appointments are for five-year terms unless the appointee fills a vacancy on the Panel, in which case they serve only the remainder of the term of the member who is replaced. The President may remove and replace any members of the FSIP at will.

The FSIP has substantial authority to resolve federal labor–management relations impasses. When collective bargaining negotiations break down, labor and management will typically ask for assistance from the Federal Mediation and Conciliation Service (FMCS). The FMCS was established as an independent federal agency under the authority of the Labor–Management Relations Act of 1947, also known as the Taft–Hartley Act. The FMCS provides labor–management mediation services in the private sector, state and local governments with collective bargaining, and in the federal sector. Mediation, as noted earlier, is a method of third-party dispute resolution in which a neutral third party (a mediator) meets with labor and management representatives individually and collectively to assist them in reaching an agreement. This kind of service is essential to bargaining wherever it occurs, but it is particularly essential in public sector jurisdictions that do not permit workers to strike.

In the federal sector, if mediation fails, the FSIP may be asked by labor and management to intervene with more direct pressure. Once the FSIP receives a request for assistance, it will conduct a preliminary investigation to determine if it should become involved by asserting jurisdiction. According to the FLRA website (https://www.flra.gov), if the FSIP does intervene, it has the authority to direct the use of various dispute resolution procedures, including informal conferences, further mediation, and fact-finding. If the impasse continues, however, the FSIP may impose a settlement for disputed contract terms at its discretion that it believes is just. This settlement is final. It is not appealable to the courts.

President Trump's Appointees to the FLRA

In the Obama years, the FLRA operated without significant controversy. During President Obama's second term, the FLRA consisted of Carol Waller Pope, a Democrat who served as Chair, Ernest DuBester, a Democrat, and Patrick Pizzella, a Republican. Pope, who had served for 20 years (1980–2000) as a career employee in the FLRA Office of General Counsel, was elevated to the Authority as a member by President Clinton at the close of his second term and later by President George W. Bush. She was first appointed Chair of the FLRA in 2009 by President Obama. In January 2017, Pope and Pizzella left the Authority before the Trump administration came in, but DuBester continued serving as the sole remaining member.

On September 5, 2017, eight months into his presidency, President Trump made two nominations to the FLRA. These individuals included Colleen D. Kiko, a Republican, to serve as Chairman of the FLRA, and James T. Abbott, a second Republican, to serve as a member. Kiko previously served as the agency's General Counsel under President George W. Bush from 2005 to 2008. Abbott had worked as a civilian attorney in the Department of the Army on labor and personnel issues. Nearly a month later, on October 3, 2017, President Trump nominated Democrat Ernest DuBester for a new term. These nominations were referred to the Senate Committee on Homeland Security and Government Affairs, Chaired at the time by Republican Senator Ron Johnson.

The Committee held a brief (1 hour) hearing on the three nominees on November 7, 2017. Senator James Lankford of Oklahoma chaired the hearing. Lankford praised all the nominees and noted their extensive experience in federal labor–management relations (U.S. Senate, 2017). The nominees, in turn, all affirmed their commitment to the right of federal employees to join labor unions and bargain collectively over terms of employment as specified in the Federal Service Labor–Management Relations Statute (U.S. Senate, 2017). Two days after the hearing, all three nominees were reported out favorably to the full Senate in a move that contrasts sharply with actions taken later by the same Senate committee regarding nominations to fill positions on the Merit Systems Protection Board. All three nominees to the FLRA were confirmed by the Senate through a voice vote on November 16, 2017, only seven days after the Committee Hearing. Interestingly, Senator Johnson and the Republicans did not attempt to confirm the nominees by unanimous consent as they would later with nominees to the MSPB. The decision to proceed with confirmation by voice vote may have meant that unanimity was lacking, and the Republicans, who controlled the Senate, chose a sure path to confirmation.

The fact that all three positions on the FLRA were filled by mid-November of 2017 did not mean that all work of the Authority could proceed from that point forward. The Office of General Counsel was vacant. As noted previously, the FLRA can hear claims of unfair labor practices only after those claims have been investigated by the General Counsel and presented to the Authority for resolution. With the General Counsel's Office vacant, no action could be taken on union appeals (or agency appeals) claiming unfair labor practices. The previous General Counsel under President Obama was Julia Clark, who served from 2009 until her departure on January 20, 2017.[4] At that point, Peter A. Sutton, the FLRA Deputy General Counsel, became Acting General Counsel and served nine months until November 16, 2017. After Sutton departed, the offices of General Counsel and Deputy General Counsel at the FLRA were both vacant.

President Trump nominated no one to fill the General Counsel vacancy until April 11, 2019, when he forwarded the name of Catherine Bird to the Senate. This nomination came 17 months after Acting General Counsel Sutton had departed. The Bird nomination was forwarded to the Senate Committee on Homeland Security and Government Affairs, Chaired by Senator Johnson of Wisconsin. The Committee held a hearing on July 16, 2019 (U.S. Senate, 2019d), and on July 24, 2019, the Committee reported Bird's nomination out favorably to the entire Senate. However, the Senate took no action, and the nomination was returned to the President on January 3, 2020. On February 12, 2020, the President renominated Catherine Bird to serve as the FLRA General Counsel, but the same pattern of events unfolded. No action was taken by the full Senate, and the nomination was returned to the President on January 3, 2021.

Consequently, the FLRA was without a General Counsel (or an Acting General Counsel) from November 16, 2017, through the end of the Trump Presidency. With no one in the General Counsel's position, the FLRA could not consider claims of unfair labor practices through the usual procedure. That aspect of the agency's responsibility was effectively curtailed. This condition meant that employees and their unions who wished to challenge perceived unfair labor practices could only file grievances that would be resolved through arbitration. The decisions of arbitrators, however, were subject to review by the Trump FLRA.

Actions of the Trump FLRA

Reversing Arbitration Decisions Favorable to Unions

As members of the Trump FLRA settled into their roles, a distinct pattern of decisions emerged. An unprecedented number of arbitration decisions favorable to federal employees and their unions were overturned when the agencies involved appealed to the FLRA, and most of those reversals were accomplished on a partisan basis, with the two Republican members Kiko and Abbott voting to overturn the arbitrator and the Democratic member DuBester dissenting.

This pattern emerged from an analysis of Trump-era FLRA decisions conducted by I. B. Helburn (Undated). Mr. Helburn was Professor Emeritus at the McCombs School of Business of the University of Texas at Austin. He was also a member of the National Academy of Arbitrators, and one of his decisions favoring a federal employee, which he regarded as well-reasoned and based on earlier FLRA case law, was overturned by the FLRA in 2018. That experience led Mr. Helburn to examine the first 30 decisions of the Trump FLRA reviewing arbitrators' decisions favorable to unions and to compare those outcomes to the last 30 decisions the FLRA had made during the George W. Bush Administration when reviewing arbitrators' decisions favorable to unions and the last thirty agency appeals made under President Obama. Mr. Helburn found that among the first 30 agency appeals considered by the Trump FLRA, 23 or 76.7 percent were overturned by the Authority – that is, the FLRA reversed the arbitration decision and ruled in favor of the agency. In 21 of those 23 reversals, Democratic member DuBester dissented, meaning the decisions were reached on a partisan basis. By comparison, only 8, or 26.7 percent, of the 30 decisions favoring the unions examined from the George W. Bush Administration were overturned, and the same result was obtained from the analysis of the decisions from the Obama FLRA. The discrepancy is striking. In addition, in 5 of the 23 cases where the Trump FLRA reversed arbitrator decisions favoring unions, the decisions overturned established FLRA precedent. No cases were examined from the Bush or Obama years were cases in which FLRA case law precedent was overturned. Furthermore, of the cases examined from the Trump period, only six resulted in FLRA decisions upholding arbitrator decisions favorable to the unions. In four of those six, the decision was reached because the agency involved failed to file an appeal within the 30-day time limit specified in the Federal Service Labor–Management Relations Statute (i.e., Title VII of the CSRA of 1978).

The actions of the Trump FLRA were reviewed at a congressional hearing held on June 4, 2019, by the House of Representatives Committee on Oversight and Reform, Subcommittee on Government Operations (U.S. House of Representatives, 2019b).[5] The FLRA Chair, Colleen Kiko, was the only witness to testify. Representative Gerald E. Connolly of Virginia chaired the Subcommittee. In an opening statement, Representative Connolly noted that

Congress had "determined by law that giving Federal workers the right to join unions and bargain collectively over their conditions of employment was 'in the public interest.'" However, the Congressman declared, "The Trump administration has made no attempt to disguise its hostility toward collective bargaining, unions, and Federal service labor laws" (U.S. House of Representatives, 2019b). In contrast to Representative Connolly's characterization, Chairman Kiko expressed her commitment to federal collective bargaining and to applying the law governing federal labor relations, the FSLMRS, in an unbiased manner.

When explicitly asked about the unprecedented increase in the number of arbitration decisions favorable to unions that were overturned under her tenure, Chairman Kiko responded that the Authority gives deference to arbitrator decisions, and those decisions are overturned only when she found that the arbitrators involved had exceeded their authority. If that is true, however, would that suggest that during the Obama and George W. Bush Administrations actions taken by arbitrators in excess of their authority were ignored? Alternatively, did the frequency with which arbitrators exceeded their authority immediately rise as the Trump Administration got underway? It stretches credulity to think that either of those possibilities is true. The fact remains that decisions by the Trump FLRA regarding arbitration awards broke sharply with the precedent set under President Obama and, even more remarkably, with the precedent set under the administration of fellow Republican George W. Bush.

Decertifying the FLRA Employee Union

Chapter 71, Subchapter II, Section 7112 of Title VII of the CSRA of 1978 specifies the FLRA's responsibilities for determining appropriate bargaining units for federal unions. The law states in part:

> "The Authority shall determine in each case whether, in order to ensure employees the fullest freedom in exercising the rights guaranteed under this chapter, the appropriate unit should be established on an agency, plant, installation, functional, or other basis and shall determine any unit to be an appropriate unit only if the determination will ensure a clear and identifiable community of interest among the employees in the unit and will promote effective dealings with, and efficiency of the operations of, the agency involved."
>
> *U.S. Congress (1978b)*

In addition, in Section 7112(b), the law outlines circumstances in which a bargaining unit is not appropriate:

> "A unit shall not be determined to be appropriate under this section solely on the basis of the extent to which employees in the proposed unit have organized, nor shall a unit be determined to be appropriate if it includes ... an employee engaged in administering the provisions of this chapter."
>
> *U.S. Congress (1978b, Section 7112(b))*

This provision, Section 7112(b), appears to exclude all employees of the FLRA from participating in unions and collective bargaining since they all are involved in administering provisions of Chapter 71 of Title VII of the CSRA of 1978. However, Section 7112(c) also specifies circumstances under which federal employees may or may not participate in a bargaining unit:

> "Any employee who is engaged in administering any provision of law relating to labor-management relations may not be represented by a labor organization – (1) which represents other individuals to whom such provision applies; or (2) which is affiliated directly or indirectly with an organization which represents other individuals to whom such provision applies."
>
> *U.S. Congress (1978b)*

This part of the law, Section 7112(c), exists to prevent the conflict of interest that would be present if a federal employee who is involved in administering provisions of labor law were represented by a union that also represents other employees subject to the law they administer or were represented by a union that is affiliated with another union that represents other employees subject to the law they administer. The conflict of interest is avoided if the union representing employees administering labor law represented no other federal employees. It seems clear that Section 7112(c) applies, for example, to employees of the National Labor Relations Board, the agency charged with overseeing labor–management relations in the private sector. Does Section 7112(c) also apply to employees of the FLRA? That is an interesting question. The provision does not explicitly exclude them, but Section 7112(b), as noted, does appear to exclude FLRA employees from collective bargaining.

Despite the language of Section 7112(b), for nearly 40 years, the FLRA, under both Republican and Democratic administrations, had recognized a union, the Union of Authority Employees, representing their workers and had negotiated employment issues and even entered into contracts with the union. The FLRA took this action under a Memorandum Opinion issued by the U.S. Department of Justice, Office of Legal Counsel under President Carter in 1980 (U.S. Department of Justice, 1980). In that opinion, the Office of Legal Counsel concluded, after a thorough review of Title VII of the CSRA of 1978 and President Nixon's Executive Order 11491, that there was nothing in the law that would preclude the FLRA from voluntarily establishing a collective bargaining system for their employees. Binding arbitration, however, could not be permitted in such a system, and any union representing FLRA employees could not also represent federal workers from other agencies (U.S. Department of Justice, 1980).

Despite this opinion issued by the Department of Justice, and despite close to four decades of FLRA experience in bargaining with its employees, Chairman Kiko announced on December 21, 2018, the date of expiration of the then-current contract with the Union of Authority Employees, that the FLRA would no longer recognize the union or any other labor organization and would not negotiate or enter into any new collective agreement with its employees (Kiko, 2018). Chairman Kiko cited Section 7112(b) of the FSLMRS to justify this decision. This decision overturned decades of practice and precedence within the FLRA.

Making It Easier for Employees to Cancel Automatic Union Dues Collection

In early 2020, the FLRA announced that it would change its interpretation of the FSLMRS to give federal employees the ability to cancel their union membership and the automatic deduction of union dues at any time, provided that it has been at least one year since they first joined the union (Wagner 2020). The actual language of the FSLMRS on this point reads as follows:

> "If an agency has received from an employee in an appropriate unit a written assignment which authorizes the agency to deduct from the pay of the employee amounts for the payment of regular and periodic dues … any such assignment may not be revoked for a period of 1 year."
>
> *U.S. Congress (1978b, Section 7115)*

This language was interpreted by the FLRA since 1981 as meaning that authorized dues deductions can only be revoked at intervals of 1 year, or more specifically during a specified 15-day period once per year negotiated by the union and agency management (7 FLRA 194, 1981).

In 2019, the U.S. Office of Personnel Management requested a general policy statement on this matter given the decision of the U.S. Supreme Court in *Janus* v. *AFSCME, Council 31* (585 U.S. ____ (2018)). In that decision, the Court ruled on First Amendment grounds that state or local public employees who are not members of a public employee union cannot be compelled to pay union dues. Such agreements for the extraction of union dues from non-members were referred to as agency shop arrangements. Proponents argued they were justified because the union had a legal obligation to represent all employees within a bargaining unit, whether they were union members or not. The provision was to prevent the "free-rider" problem for unions that occurs when employees, who are entitled to a share of all that the union negotiates, nevertheless refuse to join or support the union. Despite this, the Court ruled against the unions.

The context of federal employment, however, is quite different from the situation addressed by the Court in *Janus*. In the federal sector, there are no agency shop arrangements. Section 7102 of the FSLMRS states that employees have the right to join or assist unions or to refrain from that activity as they wish. This approach to organized labor is commonly called an open shop arrangement. Consequently, the ruling in *Janus* did not impact the collection of union dues in the federal civil service. In fact, Justice Samuel Alito, the author of the majority opinion in *Janus*, applauded the federal service for how union membership and union dues are managed. Only those federal employees who affirmatively join a union are expected to pay union dues.

Nevertheless, Chairman Kiko and Member Abbott responded to the request from OPM by reconsidering the long-standing FLRA interpretation of the law. In a decision announced on February 14, 2020, Chairman Kiko declared that the Authority now disagreed with the previous policy of the FLRA regarding employee revocation of union membership. The statement in the Statute indicating that an employee's request to have union dues withheld from his or her paycheck "may not be revoked for a period of 1 year" was to be interpreted to apply only to the first year after the initial request is made (FLRA, 2020a). After that, according to Kiko and Abbott, the employee can terminate the agreement to have union dues withheld at any time.

The argument by Kiko and Abbott is based on a reasonable interpretation of the law. As they argue in their decision, "the provision [in the statute] says that an 'assignment may not be revoked for a period of [one] year,' and such wording governs only one year because it refers to only '[one] year.'" Nevertheless, FLRA member Ernst DuBester dissented from the decision vigorously, and union leadership also raised strong objections. The new interpretation of the law, whether it was technically correct or not, clearly operated against the interests of federal employee unions.

Personnel Policy Change and the Duty to Bargain

How much of a change in personnel policy by an agency must occur for that agency to be compelled to negotiate over the implementation and impact of that change with the union representing their employees? This important question was raised by the U.S. Departments of Education and Agriculture in 2020 when they requested clarification of the issue by the FLRA.

The FSLMRS reserves to agency management the right to change "conditions of employment" defined as "personnel policies, practices, or matters ... affection working conditions" (Section 7103(a)(14)). However, the law also states in Section 7106(b):

"Nothing in this section shall preclude any agency and any labor organization from negotiating ... procedures which management officials of the agency will observe in exercising any authority under this section; or appropriate arrangements for employees adversely affected by the exercise of any authority under this section by such management officials."

U.S. Congress (1978b, Section 7106 (b))

Consequently, bargaining over the implementation and impact of agency-imposed changes in the conditions of employment, known commonly as impact bargaining, is authorized. Furthermore, it is not a concept that began following the passage of the FSLMRS in 1978. Bargaining of this nature was authorized under President Nixon's Executive Order 11491 from 1969. In those early years, and in the first years under the FSLMRS, bargaining was limited to situations where the amount of policy change was seen as substantial (FLRA, 2020b). That is, when an agency changed personnel policies, practices, or matters in a substantial way, bargaining would be required. The FLRA and, earlier, the FLRC would determine when the magnitude of change was substantial if it was disputed.

However, this policy of bargaining only over the effects of substantial change was altered by the FLRA in 1985 in favor of a policy that required bargaining over changes that were "greater than de minimis" (FLRA, 2020b). Of course, the term "de minimis" denotes a minimal or trifling change. In effect, the "greater than de minimis" standard meant that bargaining could be required whenever a change could be seen as more than trivial. A substantial impact on the conditions of employment was not required. However, disagreements emerged over the proper interpretation of "greater than de minimis" policy changes over the succeeding years. In their September 30, 2020 decision, the FLRA cited numerous conflicting interpretations. For example, in a case from 1990, the FLRA held that "rearranging [the] seating configuration within a single office [was] held to be more than de minimis," but in 1997, the Authority ruled that "moving an employee to an entirely different work location [was] held not to be more than de minimis" (FLRA, 2020b, footnote 14). In addition, in 2009, the Authority held that "requiring [an] employee to give up a 'second' office while keeping [a] primary office [was] held to be more than de minimis," but in 2012, the FLRA ruled that "moving an employee permanently to a vacant office [was] held not to be more than de minimis" (FLRA, 2020b, footnote 14).

These, and other examples of inconsistencies in interpretation of the "greater than de minimis" standard, led the Trump FLRA to conclude that "the Authority has effectively extended the bargaining obligation under the de minimis test to conclude that a matter triggers an agency's duty to bargain whenever management has made any decision, no matter how small or trivial" (FLRA, 2020b). Chairman Kiko and member Abbott continued by arguing that because the "greater than de minimis" standard "has been drained of any determinative meaning, it is now incumbent on us to reexamine and clarify when management-initiated changes have a sufficiently significant impact on conditions of employment to require bargaining" (FLRA, 2020b). Kiko and Abbott concluded that "Any standard that is used by the Authority (and concomitantly by arbitrators and judges) to determine whether a change is significant enough to warrant bargaining must draw a line that is meaningful and determinative" (FLRA, 2020b). They embraced a return to the "substantial impact" standard that had been used by the FLRA prior to 1985. Substantial impact would be the test of whether a policy change regarding a condition of employment is of sufficient magnitude to require bargaining (FLRA, 2020b).

Given the history of varying interpretations of the "greater than de minimis" standard, one could conclude that new guidance from the FLRA was needed. But the "substantial impact" standard is also subject to interpretation. Whether that standard (substantial impact) is seen as an improvement or not, the decision to reinstate it marked a significant change from earlier practice dating back to 1985. The new standard gave management greater discretion to implement personnel policy changes without dealing with the unions.

Midterm Bargaining

When labor and management initially sit down together to negotiate a collective bargaining agreement, they work to address all issues that can foreseeably arise during the full term specified for the length of their agreement. Bargaining of this nature is sometimes referred to as term bargaining. However, unforeseen issues may arise during the term of a collective bargaining agreement. Federal agencies retain authority to make decisions that may impact working conditions for employees while a contract is in effect. When this occurs, a question arises as to whether those decisions and their implementation should be negotiated with the union representing the employees. This kind of bargaining, if it is permitted, is referred to as midterm bargaining.

A question about midterm bargaining came before the FLRA in 2020 through a request for a general policy statement on the issue raised by the U.S. Office of Personnel Management (FLRA, 2020c). Specifically, OPM asked the FLRA for clarification on whether including a clause in a collective bargaining agreement that would preclude midterm bargaining is a mandatory subject of bargaining. Such a clause is known as a "zipper clause" because it zips up the agreement and closes it to any further negotiations. Zipper clauses typically state that the parties to negotiation agree that they have had the opportunity to bargain over all mandatory subjects, and they waive their rights to bargain over any matters that arise during the term of an agreement (Smith, 2022). Management generally prefers the inclusion of zipper clauses in collective bargaining agreements because it frees them from the obligation of midterm bargaining. Unions oppose zipper clauses because they would like to retain the opportunity to respond to issues not covered in initial contracts but that arise unexpectedly during the term of an agreement. Importantly, if the inclusion of zipper clauses within collective bargaining agreements is a mandatory subject of bargaining, then it is clear that the FSLMRS does not guarantee the right of federal unions to midterm bargaining.

For years, the FLRA had issued varying interpretations of the federal labor relations statute on this issue, and federal circuit courts had disagreed on what the FSLMRS required. In 1999, the U.S. Supreme Court ruled that the Statute was ambiguous on the midterm bargaining question, indicating that the FLRA should determine the matter. The following year, the FLRA responded by determining that the FSLMRS requires midterm negotiations over matters that arise during the term of a contract (FLRA 2000). That decision remained undisturbed for 20 years.

Nevertheless, on September 30, 2020, the FLRA overturned the 20-year-old precedent by ruling, at the request of OPM, that the FSLMRS does not require midterm bargaining. Whether midterm bargaining would be allowed under any specific contract was required to be negotiated as part of a term collective bargaining agreement. That is, the question of whether a zipper clause will be included within a collective bargaining agreement is a mandatory subject of bargaining. This ruling served management's interests during the Trump years because bargaining over the inclusion of a zipper clause could be negotiated to an impasse, at which point the matter could be settled through statutorily mandated impasse resolution procedures through the FSIP that had generally favored management.

Agency Head Review of Contracts under Continuance Provisions

The Federal Service Labor–Management Relations Statute provides that any contract negotiated between a union and an agency must be approved by the agency head within 30 days from the date on which agreement on the contract was reached. Agency-head approval is meant to ensure that the contract is consistent with provisions of the FSLMRS and any other laws, rules, or regulations (FSLMRS, Section 7114(c)). In addition, in Section 7116(a)(7), the Statute prohibits an agency from enforcing "any rule or regulation ... which is in conflict with any applicable collective bargaining agreement if the agreement was in effect before the date of the rule or regulation" (U.S. Congress, 1978b, p. 92, Stat at 1204).

The U.S. Department of Agriculture asked the FLRA in 2020 to issue a general statement of policy to:

> "clarify when an agency head may review the legality of an expiring agreement that includes a provision stating that, where renegotiations are requested, the existing agreement continues in force until the parties reach a new one."
>
> *FLRA(2020d)*

Specifically, the Department of Agriculture asked the FLRA to rule that when an expiring contract has a continuance clause, the agency head may review the continuing agreement as if it were a new agreement under Section 7114(c). In response, the FLRA ruled that:

> "Once a continuance provision of indefinite duration extends an agreement's operation, that newly extended agreement is, in a meaningful sense, no longer the same one that was 'in effect' before the extension occurred."
>
> *FLRA, (2020d)*

The Authority continued by saying:

"Moreover, when an agreement contains a continuance provision, parties that fail to initiate or complete renegotiations in time to reach a new agreement before the existing one expires know that such a failure will trigger the operation of the continuance provision. Therefore, by their course of conduct, those parties effectively execute a new, extended agreement when they allow the continuance provision to go into effect."

FLRA (2020d)

Accordingly, the FLRA reasoned that on the first day following the original agreement's expiration date (i.e., the first day of the "new agreement"), all government-wide regulations in effect will apply to the parties covered by the agreement, and the 30-day period for agency head approval begins. This decision would allow agency heads to unilaterally cancel contract provisions they oppose even though the parties had agreed earlier to continue their contract beyond the original expiration date. The one Democratic member of the FLRA (Ernest DuBester) strenuously dissented from the FLRA majority's ruling, reasoning that it is inconsistent with the language of the FSLMRS and arguing that "the parties to a continuance provision have mutually agreed that their existing agreement shall remain in *full force and effect* until such time as a new agreement is approved" (emphasis in original) (FLRA, 2020d). Member DuBester was making an important point. The new interpretation of the FSLMRS and the meaning of contract continuance provisions gave agency heads an unprecedented opportunity to reshape union bargaining agreements without input from the unions. That is what the FLRA majority did in this ruling, and apparently, that is what the Republican members of the FLRA wished to achieve.

Actions of the Federal Service Impasses Panel

As noted earlier in this chapter, the FSIP has the authority to issue binding decisions to settle impasses reached when collective bargaining fails. The FSIP was established as an organization housed within the FLRA, but it operates independently of the FLRA. Because FSIP decisions are not appealable, it is vitally important that the Panel be viewed as a balanced and neutral force for dispute resolution. That was, unfortunately, not how labor officials perceived the Trump Panel. After his inauguration, President Trump dismissed members of the FSIP who had served under his predecessor and appointed his own panel, as most presidents do. However, instead of selecting members with experience in labor relations and impasse resolution, Trump sought appointees with decidedly anti-union perspectives. There is, of course, no requirement that the FSIP have members from both major political parties, and all of Trump's appointees were Republicans. Randy Erwin, the President of the National Federation of Federal Employees, said in 2017 that the composition of Trump's panel reflected a "common disdain for the labor community" (Wagner, 2017). Erwin stressed further what he perceived as bias on the Panel by claiming that:

"The diversity of this panel ranges from people who publicly campaign against unions to people that actively litigate against unions. I have little faith that this panel can properly evaluate a dispute without inherent bias or personal ideology interfering."

Wagner (2017)

The presence of an FSIP with an anti-union orientation raises several concerns, including a fear that federal agencies will not negotiate in good faith and will force the creation of an impasse that may then be settled in their favor by the FSIP. This possibility was raised by the National Treasury Employees Union (NTEU) in legal action against the Department of Health and Human Services (HHS) in 2019. In this case, union officials and representatives from HHS exchanged contract proposals in June. They negotiated for only two days in July when the Department requested Federal Mediation and Conciliation Service assistance. After only two days of mediation, the Department declared an impasse and requested intervention by the FSIP. The FSIP then proceeded to issue rulings in favor of positions taken by the Department (Wagner, 2019a).

In another case, the FSIP issued rulings in May of 2019 favoring the position of the Social Security Administration (SSA) on 12 items on which the union (The American Federation of Government Employees or AFGE) and SSA had reached an impasse. Their negotiations had been ongoing for 7 months and had produced an agreement on more than 50 items. However, the agency would not yield on matters of telework and the need to limit the amount of paid time that employees who were union officials could utilize, as had been mandated by the President in one of his executive orders from May of 2018. The FSIP settled these issues in favor of the agency's position (Wagner, 2019c).

An additional decision made by the FSIP during the Trump years provided further reason to question the Panel's neutrality. This ruling, issued on January 2, 2018 also involved a dispute regarding the use of official time by employees who are union representatives (Gilson, 2018). In this case, the Panel rejected both the union and the agency proposals and instead imposed a solution of its own construction that established a limit on official time lower than either party had offered. This dispute was specifically between the United States Department of Agriculture, Office of Rural Development, and the American Federation of State, County, and Municipal Employees, Local 3870 of the Washington D.C. area.

Responses by the D.C. Circuit Court of Appeals

Decisions by the FLRA are appealable to the U.S. Court of Appeals for the District of Columbia Circuit, and between 2020 and 2022, the D.C. Circuit Court issued decisions in four cases, overturning rulings by the FLRA. The Circuit Court decided the first of these cases on June 9, 2020, in *American Federation of Government Employees* v. *Federal Labor Relations Authority*, No. 19-1069. In this case, the AFGE challenged a decision by the FLRA that overturned precedent and drew a distinction between the terms "conditions of employment" and "working conditions" as those words are used in the FSLMRS. Section 7103(a)(14) of the labor–management relations statute states: "conditions of employment" means personnel policies, practices, and matters, whether established by rule, regulation, or otherwise, affecting working conditions..." The FLRA majority argued that the terms "conditions of employment" and "working conditions" are not synonymous, but they did not explain the difference. The distinction is important because federal agencies are required under the law to notify and negotiate with unions about changes they wish to make in employees' "conditions of employment." The Authority reasoned, however, that if the two terms are distinct, an agency could issue a policy statement that affects working conditions but does not impact conditions of employment. If that occurs, such a policy statement does not constitute a change that must be subject to bargaining (70 FLRA 501 (2018)).

The case involved a memorandum issued by the Customs and Border Patrol (CBP) division chief for the El Paso, Texas sector. The memo redirected how CBP agents were to manage the inspection of vehicles entering the United States from Mexico. The AFGE filed a grievance on behalf of the agents alleging that the CBP violated the FSLMRS by changing a condition of employment without notifying and negotiating with the Union. The agency opposed the grievance, and the parties submitted the matter to arbitration, whereupon the arbitrator sided with the union and found that the memo changed agents' duties and raised safety concerns. The CBP appealed the arbitration decision to the FLRA, which, as noted, ruled that while the CBP memo changed working conditions, it did not change conditions of employment for CBP agents, and therefore, the memo did not produce a change that required notification and bargaining.

The union requested reconsideration from the FLRA, but that request was denied. The union then petitioned the D.C. Circuit Court for review. The D.C. Circuit, in a unanimous decision, vacated the FLRA decision, finding it was arbitrary and capricious. The Court ruled that:

> "If the relevant inquiry under section 7103(a)(14) is whether an agency's action constitutes a change in 'personnel policies, practices, and matters … affecting working conditions,' it would seem that a memo that affects working conditions is, by definition, a condition of employment over which the agency must bargain. The only way this would not be accurate is if the memo is not a *personnel policy, practice or matter*" (emphasis in original).
>
> *AFGE v. FLRA (2020)*

The Court also noted that prior to the FLRA decision in this case, the Authority had ruled that "there is no substantive difference between [the terms] 'conditions of employment' and 'working conditions' as those terms are practically applied" (AFGE v. FLRA, 2020) (see, 64 FLRA 85 (2009)).

The second decision by the D.C. Circuit involved a ruling by the FLRA that a proposal by the NTEU for an increase in the availability of telework for employees in the Department of Agriculture, Food and Nutrition Service was not negotiable. The case is *National Treasury Employees Union* v. *Federal Labor Relations Authority* (2021). The Trump FLRA ruled that the NTEU proposal to expand telework "violated management's right to assign work because it dictated to management when it could require employees to come to their duty stations," and it "violated management's right to direct employees because it precluded in-person supervision options" (Reardon, 2021).

A unanimous Circuit Court overturned the FLRA decision, arguing that it was arbitrary and not the product of reasoned decision-making. More specifically, the Court found that the FLRA misinterpreted the proposal made by the NTEU. The proposal acknowledged that the agency involved, the Food and Nutrition Service, could deny employee requests for telework under a variety of circumstances.

The third decision overturning the FLRA came on January 28, 2022, in *American Federation of Government Employees* v. *Federal Labor Relations*

Authority, No. 20-1398. This case was one in which the union challenged the FLRA decision regarding midterm bargaining reviewed earlier (see the section on Midterm bargaining above). The FLRA had issued a general policy statement in 2020 at the request of OPM specifying that employees and their unions have no statutory right to midterm bargaining over matters that arise unexpectedly during the term of a contract and are not covered in the contract. According to the Trump FLRA, such bargaining was permissible but not mandatory. The Authority reasoned that the question of midterm bargaining must be negotiated by labor and management. In doing so, the FLRA overturned its earlier ruling that had stood for 20 years, specifying that midterm bargaining was mandatory. Because the Authority decided that midterm bargaining was permissible but not mandatory, zipper clauses that prohibit midterm bargaining would need to be negotiated. Specifically, the issue of whether a contract should contain a zipper clause was a mandatory subject for bargaining under the FLRA's reasoning (71 FLRA 977).

The practical effect of this Trump FLRA decision was that in bargaining over the inclusion of a zipper clause, an agency could hold tight to its affirmative position and negotiate to an impasse with the union. Ultimately, then, members of the FSIP, who are political appointees, could impose a settlement including the zipper clause preferred by the agency, or even a different one that the FSIP thinks is preferable, into the contract over the union's objections. This possibility is why the union took the FLRA to Court over its policy statement on midterm bargaining.

In considering this case, the D.C. Circuit first observed that "FLRA policy statements are unusual: Before producing a spate of them in 2020, including the one challenged here, the Authority had not issued any Policy Statement *in over thirty-five years*" (emphasis added) (AFGE v. FLRA 2022). The Court then held that the FLRA ruling that the FSLMRS does not entitle employees and their union the opportunity for midterm bargaining was arbitrary and capricious. It was based on a misreading of Supreme Court precedent, and "the Authority failed to offer a reasoned explanation for its decision" (*AFGE v. FLRA*, 2022). The Authority "simply deemed it 'more appropriate' to read the Statute to not require midterm bargaining" (*AFGE* v. *FLRA*, 2022). Because the Authority's holding that midterm bargaining was permissive but not mandatory was arbitrary and unsupported by the text of the FSLMRS, the FLRA ruling that declared zipper clauses are mandatory subjects for bargaining was equally unsound (*AFGE* v. *FLRA*, 2022). Consequently, the D.C. Circuit Court voted without dissent to vacate the entirety of the FLRA policy statement on midterm bargaining.

The fourth ruling of the D.C. Circuit overturned, again by a unanimous vote, the FLRA decision allowing the heads of agencies to review contracts that were automatically extended by mutual agreement when the initial term expired (see the section above on Agency Head Review of Contracts Under Continuance Provisions). This decision of the FLRA (2020d) gave agency heads the power to unilaterally cancel contract provisions despite the fact that the parties had agreed in advance to continue living under the contract. Rules and regulations issued since the contract was initially confirmed would also be applied. Soon after the FLRA policy statement was issued, the NTEU petitioned the Court of Appeals for the D.C. Circuit for a ruling.

The case was *National Treasury Employees Union* v. *Federal Labor Relations Authority*, decided on August 2, 2022. The Court began its analysis by observing that the federal labor relations statute (the FSLMRS) permits an agency head to review a collective bargaining agreement before it takes effect to determine if the agreement conflicts with applicable federal law (Section 7114(c)(1)). If there is no conflict with existing law, the agency head must approve the agreement (Section 7114(c)(2)).[6] The Court also observed that the FSLMRS forbids agencies from enforcing regulations, that conflict with a collective bargaining agreement, which were issued after the agreement took effect (*NTEU* v. *FLRA,* 2022, p. 3). The question before the Court was:

> "whether the triggering of a continuance clause, which extends a contract pending negotiations of a successor agreement, permits a second round of agency-head review and enforcement of conflicting regulations that became effective after the original agreement."
>
> *NTEU v. FLRA (2022, p. 3)*

The FLRA had reasoned that a bargaining agreement extended under a continuance clause was essentially a new agreement and that agency head review was therefore required, and the contract must conform to conflicting regulations. The D.C. Circuit overturned the FLRA on both points. The Court determined that a continuance clause "manifests the parties' intent to be bound by the terms of their *original* agreement pending further negotiations" (emphasis in original) (*NTEU v. FLRA,* 2022, p. 7). Consequently, the operation of a continuance clause does not establish a new agreement; it simply signals a continuation of the previous agreement until a new contract is negotiated. Therefore, a new agency-head review is not permitted, and enforcement of regulations established after the agreement originally took effect, and that conflict with the agreement, may not occur.

Conclusion

It is clear from the foregoing discussion that the FLRA dramatically changed direction during the Administration of President Donald J. Trump. When Republican Chairman Colleen D. Kiko and her Republican colleague James T. Abbott were confirmed, they set out to reverse several previous actions the Authority had taken, even under earlier Republican presidents. Decisions by the FLRA were usually made on the basis of 2 to 1 votes, with the Democratic Member Ernest DuBester dissenting. The Authority frequently overturned arbitration decisions favoring labor and the unions. They decertified the union representing their own employees. The Authority also ended the automatic collection of union dues. They issued policy statements overturning their own precedents that had been in place in some instances from the earliest years of the FLRA's operation.

In these instances, the Trump FLRA preferred positions taken by federal agencies and their leaders over the interests of federal employees and their unions. The Authority sought to limit collective bargaining whenever possible and to expand managerial discretion. It is not unfair to say that the actions of the FLRA placed the unions at a disadvantage. The failure to fill the position of General Counsel at the FLRA and actions taken by the FSIP are consistent with this orientation. One should certainly expect that when the leadership of an organization, such as the FLRA, changes to reflect a change in political party affiliation of the President, we will see that organization chart a different course. That is an outcome consistent with political accountability within a democracy. However, the kinds of changes undertaken by the FLRA during the Trump years were at the edge of the normal distribution. The policies of the FLRA under President Trump were consistent with an administration interested in constraining the power of federal employee unions and augmenting the authority of the President to direct the executive branch of government.

Notes

1 As noted in Chapter 4, *supra*, one may question the constitutionality of the FSLMRS (Title VII of the CSRA). The FLRA itself was established by presidential action through President Carter's Reorganization Plan No. 2 of 1978. The FSLMRS was included in the CSRA to amend Title 5 of the U.S. Code to reflect Carter's reorganization, as was noted earlier in Chapter 3, *supra*. However, the FSLMRS specifies details of federal collective bargaining that had previously rested on presidential Executive Order. Whether Congress may mandate implementation of that policy and

thereby restrict presidential authority within the executive branch is an interesting issue that has yet to be litigated.

2 Labor–management relations in the Postal Service have been organized and operated separately since the passage of the Postal Reorganization Act of 1970, which established the Postal Service as an independent federal government corporation and gave postal employees full collective bargaining rights, including the right to bargain over wages and benefits. See endnote 1 from Chapter 6, *supra.*

3 The language of the Statute uses the term "Chairman," and thus, that title is applied even when women head the FLRA.

4 After Julia Clark left the position of General Counsel at the FLRA on January 20, 2017, she later assumed the position of Deputy General Counsel at the Congressional Office of Compliance, a congressional agency responsible for protecting workplace rights of employees working for the legislative branch. See Chapter 3, *supra,* for a discussion of Clark's subsequent nomination to serve as a Merit Systems Protection Board member.

5 In addition to reviewing the reversal of arbitration decisions favorable to unions, the Subcommittee also questioned Chairman Kiko about the closing of FLRA regional offices in Boston and Dallas, the precipitous drop in FLRA employee job satisfaction during her tenure, and the elimination of collective bargaining rights for FLRA employees.

6 The FSLMRS specifies that if an agency head does not act to approve or disapprove an agreement within 30 days of its execution, the agreement takes effect and is binding on labor and management (Section 7114(c)(3)).

8

THE RISK TO EXPERTISE

Who makes federal public policy? If you respond to this question by as-serting that the U.S. Congress makes policies through the legislative pro-cess, you would be correct. Congress passes legislation to authorize public programs and to appropriate the money necessary to implement those pro-grams. Congress also oversees the actions of federal departments and agen-cies. However, if you indicate that the President makes federal policies, you would also be correct. The President assists in the legislative process by advocating for specific bills, signing bills into law, and occasionally vetoing legislation. The President also issues executive orders and appoints top-level officials to direct federal departments and agencies. You could also respond to the question above by indicating that the Courts make policy. That re-sponse is correct as well. The courts, especially the U.S. Supreme Court, make policy by judging whether measures passed by Congress or actions taken by the President or by federal departments and agencies are consistent with the U.S. Constitution or statutory law. All three branches of the federal government make public policy.

There is, however, another essential actor in the policy process: The bu-reaucracy. The bureaucracy encompasses all of the various federal depart-ments and agencies within the executive branch of the government. These organizations are established to implement laws and programs, and the power to implement includes the power to make decisions that give form to the op-eration of policies and programs. Implementation is the process through which

DOI: 10.4324/9781032656380-8

plans and directives are translated into the day-to-day functioning of program activities. Government policies become real through the implementation process. Those working within the bureaucracy are given discretion to use their expertise to fill in details during the implementation process to respond to issues that arise that were not foreseen when programs were first authorized. In addition, employees from federal departments and agencies work with and advise members of Congress and congressional committees as legislation is being drafted and considered. Many agencies also issue rules and regulations that govern segments of our economy, and they ensure the functioning of the government on a daily basis. The "bureaucracy" thus plays a significant role in the public policy process. This fact has long been recognized and has consumed the intellectual energy of countless public policy and administration scholars for decades (see, e.g., Meier and Bohte, 2007; Rourke, 1965, 1968; Simon, 1947; Waldo, 1948).

Employees working within the departments and agencies of the executive branch are given discretionary authority to help shape public policy for two reasons. The first is the incapacity of the political branches of government. For example, neither the Congress nor the President can identify and address every circumstance or detailed problem that may arise in policy or program implementation (see Chapter 1, *supra*). As a result, discretion must be assigned to the bureaucrats. However, the assignment of discretionary authority to administrative agencies is eased by the fact that employees within those agencies have expertise in substantive policy areas, and often, these civil servants have a monopoly on expertise in specific fields. This is the second reason that employees in federal agencies are given administrative discretion. Bureaucratic expertise means that employees and the agencies they work in have the knowledge, skills, and abilities to get things done.

In addition, as Francis Rourke (1968) noted decades ago, the power of bureaucrats varies with the nature of their expertise, the degree to which they can monopolize that expertise, and the extent to which we desire what their expertise can deliver. Bureaucrats also have clients, i.e., members of the public who benefit from what they do. Those clients will protect the discretion and authority of bureaucrats in order to keep their benefits flowing. The higher the status and the greater the resources of bureaucratic clients, the greater the support they can provide (Rourke, 1968).

As a consequence of this context, administrative discretion can never be entirely eliminated, nor would we want that to happen. Administrative expertise facilitates the operation of public programs and provides justification for administrative discretion. But administrative expertise creates a core problem for government accountability. In an excellent book on the need for expertise in government, Don Kettl (2023) described the dilemma well:

> "The fundamental, eternal paradox about experts in government is this: it is impossible to implement complicated government programs, from roads to national defense, without experts. However, expert knowledge inevitably creates its own political power and instability, because it is always hard for government leaders to know enough to keep that power in check."
>
> *Kettl (2023, p. 1)*

In short, we need expertise in the administrative agencies of government, and as the complexity of the problems that the government addresses has grown more prominent, the need for expertise has increased. Consider, for example, the complex work of the Nuclear Regulatory Commission regarding the safe use and storage of radioactive materials. Alternatively, think about the Securities and Exchange Commission's responsibility to regulate securities markets and protect the interests of investors. The Food and Drug Administration faces a similarly complex job as it works to ensure the purity and safety of food and medicines. The work of the Environmental Protection Agency is difficult as well and rests on scientific knowledge, as do the efforts of the Centers for Disease Control and Prevention to protect public health. Tasks performed by the Department of Homeland Security are equally complicated and important, as is the work of the National Weather Service, as we have discussed. Virtually all federal agencies address complex or "wicked" problems (see Ferlie, Fitzgerald, McGivern, Dopson and Bennett, 2011).

However, as Kettl (2023) notes, our need for and reliance on expertise makes it increasingly difficult for elected politicians to control the bureaucracy effectively. Moreover, the problem of bureaucratic control is compounded by the operation of the merit system. That system is designed to ensure that federal employees are hired based on expertise (i.e., merit), and it simultaneously erects obstacles to political control by requiring, among other things, procedural due process in terminations and other limitations on managerial prerogative. We are, thus, confronted with a tension between a desire for democratic government and political accountability on one hand and constraints placed on political control of the bureaucracy by civil service laws and the exercise of expertise by bureaucrats.

Conservative politicians and their advisors today desire greater political control to push the federal bureaucracy in their preferred policy directions, which include, among other things, a reduction in the federal regulatory burden.

This objective is what the actions taken during the Trump Administration regarding personnel policy and the merit system were about. And as we have seen, most of that action was well within the President's constitutional authority. That is precisely why the federal merit system is fragile. However, if merit is eroded and political loyalty is the new currency, expertise within the federal service may be diminished or subordinated to political impulse.

The successful implementation of policies concerning the civil service pursued by the Trump Presidency from 2017 to 2021, and likely to be reimplemented in a future Republican Administration, could have three significantly adverse effects on expertise in government.[1] First, the policies may drive experts from federal employment, especially those that are close to retirement and have years of experience and institutional knowledge. A loss of that nature could be extraordinarily harmful. Second, employees that remain may be less likely to voice their views when they know their opinions are unwelcome. Under a new version of Schedule F, federal workers with policy responsibility may suppress their opinions rather than risk termination or other sanctions. They will be likely to remain quiet and loyal to the political regime. And finally, students with scientific skill and expertise obtained from degree programs in our best colleges and universities may find employment in the federal civil service unattractive. Thus, it will be difficult to replace highly skilled federal workers who leave the service. These possibilities are real, and they should be a matter of concern. We need experts to confront complex policy issues – even when they recommend decisions disfavored by a President or members of Congress. Indeed, one might conclude that experts are needed, particularly in those circumstances. Still, the pressure the Trump Administration placed on the civil service was oriented to produce bureaucratic acquiescence and loyalty to the President's political agenda even when professional expertise would lead in a different direction.

Today, there are numerous politicians, conservative policymakers, and legal scholars that are dedicated to changes that will overturn core aspects of the merit system. Examples of their ideas are found in statements and policy papers from the Heritage Foundation (e.g., Dans and Groves, 2023; Heritage Foundation, 2017; Muhlhausen, 2017, 2017b) and in the writings of analysts such as Philip K. Howard (2017). James Sherk of the America First Policy Institute is another articulate spokesperson for these views. Sherk served in the Trump Administration on the White House Domestic Policy Council and advocated in carefully reasoned essays for reforms to make the dismissal of federal workers easier and for the implementation of Schedule F (see, e.g., a statement on these positions in Sherk, 2021). Sherk was the architect of President Trump's Executive Orders of May 25, 2018, and the President's Executive Order establishing Schedule F (Sherk, 2022).

Reforms advocated by James Sherk and others and implemented during the Trump years illustrate the kinds of transformations that opponents of traditional concepts of merit wish to impose. Given his background and experience, it is unlikely that President Trump was knowledgeable of issues associated with the history of the civil service or its operation. But elections are never simply about bringing a particular candidate to office. There is always a coalition of interests associated with the candidate that also comes to power. The people President Trump brought into his Administration were knowledgeable and pressed hard for the kinds of changes to the merit system that the Administration pursued. President Trump was responsive to their arguments, and the changes sought generally fell within the scope of his authority.

The constraints that the federal merit system places on political control include limitations on who can enter the system and limitations on how people are removed from the system. Merit requires that the vast majority of employees in government be selected in a politically neutral manner based on demonstrated competence. According to this perspective, politicians should not dictate who fills the offices in government except for leadership positions in higher levels of the bureaucracy. Coupled with this idea is the equally important principle that politicians should not be able to remove public employees for political reasons – except for those employees who are politically appointed. Van Riper (1958) described these two ideas as strategies for controlling the "front door" to public service (i.e., selection based on open and competitive examination) and efforts to control the "back door" (i.e., limitations on removals). Van Riper noted that the framers of the Pendleton Act "consistently emphasized that, if the *front-door* were properly tended, the *back-door* would take care of itself" (Van Riper, 1958, p. 102). They argued that if politicians cannot appoint whomever they want, there is less incentive to remove people for inappropriate reasons. Despite the logic of this line of reasoning, in the years following the Pendleton Act, the back door was strengthened, as we have seen by Executive Orders from Presidents McKinley and Theodore Roosevelt, the Lloyd–LaFollette Act of 1912, and rulings by the United States Supreme Court mandating procedural due process in civil service removals when employees have been promised that dismissal will be for just cause only (see, Van Riper, 1958, pp. 144 and 217, Executive Order 101, Executive Order 371, Lloyd–LaFollette Act 1912, and *Cleveland Board of Education* v. *Loudermill* 1985).

Notably, the policies initiated during the Trump years regarding the federal civil service sought to weaken both doors to the public service. Schedule F, for example, made it easier for political leaders and their appointees to control employee selection by moving large segments of the workforce into the Excepted Service. Simultaneously, Trump's order creating Schedule F also eased restrictions on removal for employees in Schedules A, C, D, E, and F of the Excepted Service. That change meant that removal could be accomplished more efficiently, with less concern for due process, and removal, or perhaps more accurately the threat of removal, would compel employees to follow political dictates more faithfully.

The other central area of emphasis within the Trump reforms (besides making employee termination easier) was the attack on public employee unions. One could ask why the assault on the unions was pressed so strenuously, especially considering that federal employee unions are relatively weak by standard measures of union strength. They are prohibited by law from negotiating wages, benefits, and a broad array of workplace issues. But the unions are strong advocates for employees and principles of merit, and they work to oppose the kinds of changes that threaten their members and the merit system. Union grievance procedures are available for employees to challenge specific personnel management actions including termination. In addition, the unions may bring legal challenges against administrative reforms, as was done in response to Trump's Executive Orders from May of 2018 and in response to actions by the Trump FLRA. Federal employee rights to union membership and collective bargaining were established by presidential initiative and are grounded today in statutory law, but the President retains substantial influence over bargaining procedures and the way unions work in the federal service. Conservative Presidents see the unions as obstacles to the exercise of their power and the realization of their policy goals, and it does not help, of course, that political donations from federal employee unions are overwhelmingly distributed to support Democrats (Smith, 2021).

The conservative argument draws on principles of democracy and accountability to elected officials. They make a valid point. We must find a way of resolving the tension between expertise and political control. One approach to this puzzle is to remember that we should be working to control bureaucratic power – not end it. We can constrain the administrative state through application of the powers of the countervailing branches of government and scrutiny from the press and the public – all strategies well-established and grounded in the rule of law. For example, as noted above, Congress authorizes policies and programs and controls agency budgets. Congress also provides oversight – a practice can and should be strengthened. The Senate approves nominations of individuals to the highest-ranking positions. That process, while it is political, should be made more efficient. The President makes appointments of individuals to direct departments and agencies and helps to guide the budget process. The Courts rule on the legality of administrative actions. There is an enormous body of administrative law that guides agencies, and the procedures by which agencies issue regulations are detailed and thorough, requiring careful thought and justification for agency action. The press also helps expose abuse or corruption, and administrators are expected to follow professional and ethical norms. These are all avenues through which we achieve significant measures of control. However, even when these mechanisms are considered collectively, they cannot eliminate administrative discretion. Government agencies will still exercise discretionary authority based on expertise – as they should.

This truth, coupled with the complexity of much that the government does, makes it imperative that the federal workforce be staffed with people who act on the basis of politically neutral competence. Employees' decisions should be based on expert knowledge, and they should be loyal to the Constitution and federal statutory law rather than to any particular party or politician. Approximately 140 years ago, with passage of the Pendleton Act of 1883, the United States decided to establish such a system – to develop a capable and professional public service selected on merit principles and protected from partisan abuse. The civil service merit system shields the public bureaucracy from political control by placing constraints on how employees are hired and dismissed. If you are interested in expanding political control of the public workforce, especially control by the President who is constitutionally the head of the executive branch, certain provisions of the merit system may be seen as obstacles. That was the view of people in the Trump Administration, and it continues to be the view of many important and influential supporters of former President Trump today.

The fledgling merit system of 1883 was nurtured gradually and sustained. Over the years, it became the primary mechanism for filling jobs in the federal workforce. For decades, there was a broad consensus that merit should be the foundation for public service. Indeed, that consensus was generally considered unshakable. Nevertheless, as we have seen, the merit system is vulnerable to attack. There are many virtues of the structures erected to secure merit. Among them are the promotion of competence in government and commitment to the rule of law rather than to any particular presidential administration (Aberbach and Rockman, 2023). The system helps to ensure competence, stability, continuity, and order. These are essential values. However, the Constitution places enormous authority in the President, and the merit system will not endure unless our consensus on its underlying principles is upheld and we maintain a general agreement that we will abide by those principles. If the merit system is eroded, expertise within the bureaucracy will also be diminished or eroded. Expertise will be made subordinate to political loyalty. This risk to expertise is what is at stake in our system of government.

The election of President Biden ended the implementation of most of the civil service changes initiated during the Trump years. While Biden's reversal of the Trump reforms was a victory for merit, the risk to the system is still present. But the structure and operation of the civil service is not an issue with which most ordinary citizens are concerned. Most people are unaware of the issues involved, and they certainly do not vote based on politicians' positions on the civil service. Most members of the public simply do not know what is going on concerning the public service, and they are uninterested. The average citizen was undoubtedly unaware that the work of the MSPB was curtailed during the Trump years. These same people were likely unconcerned with the Trump Administration's effort to limit collective bargaining with federal employees and the use of "official time" by employees who serve as union officers. The dismantling of the U.S. Office of Personnel Management was not a concern. Implications of the potential transfer of tens of thousands of federal workers into an employment category in the Excepted Service were not understood by most citizens. It is certainly also the case that actions taken by the FLRA to overturn decades of precedent regarding labor policy and to substantially expand federal agency heads' power to alter collective bargaining agreements unilaterally were not matters of great apprehension. This situation is unfortunate because it allows proponents of dramatic reform to continue to press their agendas with little public outcry.

Advocates for the reforms initiated by President Trump are at work today as tirelessly as ever. Former officials of the Trump Administration and Republican members of the U.S. House of Representatives have recently argued that if Trump wins the White House in 2024, they will push their plans for the civil service forward again with even greater vigor (Ogrysko, 2021d; Swan 2022a, 2022b; Wagner, 2022a, 2022b). The Heritage Foundation has publicized an explicit agenda for reinstating Trump's policies – known as "Project 2025" (Dans and, Groves, 2023). If the Republicans gain control of the Senate in the fall of 2024, those advocating for change in the civil service will have potent allies among the Chairs of key Senate committees, especially the Committee on Homeland Security and Governmental Affairs. Today, there is most assuredly a breakdown in our historic agreement on how the civil service should operate.

If that consensus remains fractured, the concept of merit in public employment, as we have known it, will remain in peril. In an insightful article on the Trump Presidency and the federal bureaucracy, political scientist Bert Rockman notes that the neglect or downgrading of merit and efforts to elevate personal loyalty to the President during the Trump years were tools to delegitimize government, damage neutral competence, and facilitate an authoritarian conquest of the civil service (Rockman, 2019, p. 26). As Rockman explains, a public bureaucracy with a measure of independence is essential for the rule of law (Rockman, 2019, p. 14). The reforms initiated under Trump, however, were oriented toward a different objective – political loyalty.

At-will employment, a "reform" that has long been discussed and implemented in several states, can weaken the ability of the civil service to serve as a check on presidential behavior (Moynihan, 2021). Consequently, at-will employment and other threats to merit can impair government effectiveness when combined with a devaluing of administrative capability. This reform is driven by conservative politicians and analysts who wish to have more complete political control of the federal workforce. Proponents of Trump-style reforms often argue that dismissal is much easier in the private sector than in government. While technically accurate, that argument is overstated, as Kettl (2020a) demonstrated. The dismissal of employees is generally not a pleasant exercise, whether in the private or public sector, and public administration occurs within an overtly political environment. Given this context, why should it be easier than it is currently to fire public employees? Under the current system, employees *are* removed for cause. What motivation is there for this reform except a wish to remove, or threaten to remove, employees who are perceived, for one reason or another, as insufficiently loyal to political leadership?

Ultimately, the reforms implemented by President Trump and advocated for by Republicans generally are not about good management but are instead about finding ways to make the federal workforce more directly answerable to the President in order to weaken government agencies and programs that are disfavored. *What is needed to oppose that kind of action is a new consensus on the value of merit in public employment to ensure the presence of competent, qualified, and dedicated public servants who can perform their tasks without fear of political interference or retaliation.*

In the 1990s, the reinventing government movement and the concept of "new public management" rested in part on the assumption that you can deregulate public personnel administration through dramatic reforms intended to increase "managerial flexibility" because politicians had fully accepted merit principles and recognized the importance of politically neutral competence in the public workforce. The rise of right-wing populism and the Trump Presidency proved this assumption to be fundamentally wrong.[2] Administrative reforms are usually grounded on political motives and, at the federal level, are almost always oriented toward augmenting presidential control (Rockman, 2019). The federal merit system was initiated and developed to promote the growth of administrative expertise required for effective government. It is imperiled today, and government expertise and capacity are at risk. In considering these issues, one should contemplate this question: "Who should forecast the pathways of hurricanes?"

Notes

1 These ideas are consistent with the arguments of Albert O. Hirschman in his classic work on options available to organizational members who are dissatisfied with policies or management of their organizations. Hirschman's book is entitled: *Exit, Voice, and Loyalty: Responses to Decline in Firms, Organizations, and States* (Cambridge, Massachusetts: Harvard University Press, 1970).

2 This is an astute observation made to the author by Professor Frank J. Thompson of Rutgers University after Professor Thompson read an early draft of this manuscript.

REFERENCES

Aberbach, Joel D. and Bert A. Rockman. 2023. "The United States: The Political Context of Administrative Reform." In Shaun Goldfinch, ed. *The Handbook of Administrative Reform*, second edition. (Cheltenham, UK: Edward Elgar Publishers).

Alexander, Sheldon and Marian Ruderman. 1987. "The Role of Procedural and Distributive Justice in Organizational Behavior." *Social Justice Research*, Vol. 1, pp. 177–198.

American Federation of Government Employees v. *Federal Labor Relations Authority*, No. 19-1069 (D.C. Cir. 2020).

American Federation of Government Employees v. *Federal Labor Relations Authority*, No. 20-1398 (D.C. Cir. 2022).

Arnold, Peri E. 1998. *Making the Managerial Presidency: Comprehensive Reorganization Planning 1905–1996*, second edition. (Lawrence, KS: University Press of Kansas).

Battaglio, R. Paul Jr 2015. *Public Human Resource Management: Strategies and Practices for the 21st Century*. (Thousand Oaks, CA: CQ Press).

Bellamy, Jay. 2016. "A Stalwart of Stalwarts: Garfield's Assassin See Deed as a Special Duty." *Prologue Magazine*, Vol. 48, No. 3. (Washington, D.C.: U.S. National Archives).

Berman, Evan M., James S. Bowman, Jonathan P. West and Montgomery R. Van Wart. 2022. *Human Resource Management in Public Service: Paradoxes, Processes, and Problems*, seventh edition. (Thousand Oaks, CA: CQ Press).

Brands, H. W. 2005. *Andrew Jackson: His Life and Times*. (New York: Doubleday).

Brewer, Gene A., J. Edward Kellough and Hal G. Rainey. 2022. "The Importance of Merit Principles for Civil Service Systems: Evidence from the U.S. Federal Sector." *Review of Public Personnel Administration*, Vol. 42, No. 4, pp. 686–708.

Brice-Saddler, Michael. 2019. "While Bemoaning Mueller Probe, Trump Falsely Says the Constitution Gives Him 'The Right to Do Whatever I Want.'" *The Washington Post*. (July 23, 2019).

Cayer, N. Joseph and Meghna Sabharwal. 2016. *Public Personnel Administration: Managing Human Capital*, sixth edition. (San Diego, CA: Birkdale Publishers).

Chappellet-Lanier, Tajha. 2019. "Weichert Makes Her Case for the OPM Reorganization." *Fedscoop.* (May 15, 2019). Accessed at: https://www.fedscoop.com/weichert-makes-case-opm-reorganization/

Cleveland Board of Education v. *Loudermill.* 470 U.S. 532. 1985.

Crouch, Jeffrey P., Mark J. Rozell and Mitchel A. Sollenberger 2020. *The Unitary Executive: A Danger to Constitutional Government.* (Lawrence, KS: University of Kansas Press).

Dans, Paul and Steven Groves. 2023. *Mandate for Leadership: The Conservative Promise, Project 2025.* (Washington, D.C.: The Heritage Foundation).

Devine, Donald J 2017. *Political Management of the Bureaucracy: A Guide to Reform and Control.* (Ottawa, IL: Jameson Books).

Erik McKinley, Eriksson. 1927. "The Federal Civil Service under President Jackson." *The Mississippi Valley Historical Review*, Vol. 13, No. 4 (March), pp. 517–540. https://doi.org/10.2307/1892462

Executive Order 101. 1897. "Amending Civil Service Rules Regarding Removal from Service." President William McKinley. (July 27, 1897). Accessed at: https://en.wikisource.org/wiki/Executive_Order_101

Executive Order 371. 1905."Amending Civil Service Rule XII, Pertaining to Removal." President Theodore Roosevelt. (November 17, 1905). Accessed at: https://en.wikisource.org/wiki/Executive_Order_371

Federal Labor Relations Authority (FLRA). 2000. *Decision and Order on Remand.* (56 FLRA no. 6: February 28, 2000). Accessed at: https://www.flra.gov/decisions/v56/56-006.html

Federal Labor Relations Authority (FLRA). 2020a. *Decision on Request for General Statement.* (71 FLRA no. 107: February 14, 2020). Accessed at: https://www.flra.gov/decisions/v71/71-107.html

Federal Labor Relations Authority (FLRA). 2020b. *Decision on Request for General Statement.* (71 FLRA No. 190: September 30, 2020). Accessed at: https://www.flra.gov/decisions/v71/71-190.html

Federal Labor Relations Authority (FLRA). 2020c. *Decision on Request for General Statement.* (71 FLRA No. 191: September 30, 2020). Accessed at: https://www.flra.gov/decisions/v71/71-191.html

Federal Labor Relations Authority (FLRA). 2020d. *Decision on Request for General Statement.* (71 FLRA No. 192: September 30, 2020). Accessed at: https://www.flra.gov/decisions/v71/71-192.html

Federal Register. 2017. "Executive Order 13781: Comprehensive Plan for Reorganizing the Executive Branch." *Federal Register*, Vol. 82, No. 50, pp. 13959–13960. (March 16, 2017).

Federal Register. 2018a. "Executive Order 13836: Developing Efficient, Effective, and Cost-Reducing Approaches to Federal Sector Collective Bargaining." *Federal Register*, Vol. 83, No. 106, pp. 25329–25334. (June 1, 2018).

Federal Register. 2018b. "Executive Order 13837: Ensuring Transparency, Accountability, and Efficiency in Taxpayer-Funded Union Time Use." *Federal Register*, Vol. 83, No. 106, pp. 25335–25340. (June 1, 2018).

Federal Register. 2018c. "Executive Order 13839: Promoting Accountability and Streamlining Removal Procedures Consistent With Merit Principles." *Federal Register*, Vol. 83, No. 106, pp. 25343–25347. (June 1, 2018)

Federal Register. 2020. "Executive Order 13957: Creating Schedule F in the Excepted Service." *Federal Register*, Vol. 85, No. 106, pp. 67631–67635. (October 21, 2020).

Ferlie, Ewan, Louise Fitzgerald, Gerry McGivern, Sue Dopson and Chris Bennett. 2011. "Public Policy Networks and 'Wicked Problems:' A Nascent Solution?" *Public Administration*, Vol. 89, No. 2, pp. 307–324.

Fisher, Louis. 1998. *The Politics of Shared Power: Congress and the Executive*, fourth edition. (College Station, TX: Texas A&M University Press).

Freedman, A. and J. Samenow. (2020). "NOAA Leaders Violated Agency's Scientific Integrity Policy, Hurricane Dorian 'Sharpiegate' Investigation Finds." Washington Post (June 15), www.washingtonpost.com/weather/2020/06/15/noaa-investigation-sharpiegate/

Gilson Bob. 2018. "Impasses Panel Signals Policy Shift: Want It? Prove You Need It! Fedsmith.com (February 1, 2018). Accessed at: https://www.fedsmith.com/2018/01/25/impasses-panel-signals-policy-shift-want-prove-need/

Helburn, I. B. Undated. "The Trump FLRA: Fair or Foul?" Accessed at: https://cdn.govexec.com/media/gbc/docs/pdfs_edit/060619ew1.pdf

Heritage Foundation. 2017. "Reorganizing the Federal Government: What Needs to Be Done and How to Do It." The Heritage Foundation Panel. (August 2017). Accessed at: https://www.heritage.org/government-regulation/event/reorganizing-the-federal-government-what-needs-be-done-and-how-do-it.

HIAS (Hebrew Immigrant Aid Society). 2022. Mark Cohen.

Hirschman, Albert O. 1970. *Exit, Voice, and Loyalty: Responses to Decline in Firms, Organizations, and States*. (Cambridge, Massachusetts: Harvard University Press).

Hogue, Henry B. 2012. *Presidential Reorganization Authority: History, Recent Initiatives, and Options for Congress*. (Washington D.C.: Congressional Research Service).

Hopkins, Deborah, 2019. "Two MSPB Nominees Voted Out of Committee, but Uncertainty Still Looms." *Federal Employment Law Training Group Newsletter*. (February 13, 2019). Accessed at: https://feltg.com/two-mspb-nominees-voted-out-of-committee-but-uncertainty-still-looms/

Howard, Philip K. 2017. "Civil Service Reform: Reassert the President's Constitutional Authority." *The American Interest*. (January 28, 2017). Accessed at: https://www.the-american-interest.com/2017/01/28/civil-service-reform-reassert-the-presidents-constitutional-authority/

Howell, William and Terry Moe. 2021. "Big Government Vastly Expanded Presidential Power. Republicans Use It to Sabotage the Administrative State." *The Washington Post*. (November 1, 2021). Accessed at: https://www.washingtonpost.com/

politics/2021/11/01/big-government-vastly-expanded-presidential-power-republicans-use-it-sabotage-administrative-state/

J. W. Hampton, Jr. & Co. v. United States, 276 U.S. 394. 1928.

Joint Committee on Printing, United States Congress. 2020. *Official Congressional Directory 116th Congress*, 2019–2021, p. 382. Accessed at: https://www.govinfo.gov/app/collection/cdir/cdir_116/2020-07-22

Judicial Nomination Commission, 2024. "Mark A. Robbins." Accessed at: https://jnc.dc.gov/biography/mark-robbins

Katz, Eric. 2018. "MSPB Likely to Remain Powerless as Senate Panel Fails to Advance Trump's Nominees." *Government Executive*. (November 28). Accessed at: https://www.govexec.com/pay-benefits/2018/11/mspb-likely-remain-powerless-senate-panel-fails-advance-trumps-nominees/153100/

Katz, Eric. 2019. "Senate Panel Advances Merit Board, FEMA Administrator Nominees," *Government Executive*. (June 19, 2019). Accessed at: https://www.govexec.com/management/2019/06/senate-panel-advances-final-mspb-fema-administrator-nominees/157857/print/

Katz, Eric. 2021. "Federal Employee Appeals Board Nominees Preview How They Will Reduce Case Backlog." *Government Executive*. (September 22, 2021). Accessed at: https://www.govexec.com/workforce/2021/09/federal-employee-appeals-board-nominees-preview-how-they-will-reduce-backlog-handle-vaccine-mandate-challenges/185526/

Kaufman, Herbert. 1956. "Emerging Conflicts in the Doctrines of Public Administration." *American Political Science Review*, Vol. 50, No. 4, pp. 1057–1073.

Kellough, J. Edward and Lloyd G. Nigro. 2000. "Civil Service Reform in Georgia: Going to the Edge?." *Review of Public Personnel Administration*, Vol. 20, No. 4, pp. 41–54.

Kellough, J. Edward and Lloyd G. Nigro. 2006. "Dramatic Reform of the Civil Service: At-Will Employment and the Creation of a New Public Workforce." *Journal of Public Administration Research and Theory*, Vol. 16, No. 3, (July), pp. 447–466.

Kettl, Donald F. 2020a. "Schedule F Order Relies on a Myth the Private Sector Fires More People Than the Government." *Government Executive* (November 2, 2020). Accessed at: https://www.govexec.com/management/2020/11/schedule-f-order-relies-myth-private-sector-fires-more-people-government/169730/

Kettl, Donald F. 2020b. "Trump's Order Sets the Stage for Loyalty Tests for Thousands of Feds." *Government Executive*. (October 22, 2020). Accessed at: https://www.govexec.com/management/2020/10/trumps-order-sets-stage-loyalty-tests-thousands-feds/169492/

Kettl, Donald F. 2023. *Experts in Government: The Deep State from Caligula to Trump and Beyond*. (Cambridge, UK: Cambridge University Press).

Kim, Jungin and J. Edward Kellough. 2014. "At-Will Employment in the States: Examining the Perceptions of Agency Personnel Directors." *Review of Public Personnel Administration*, Vol. 34, No. 3, pp. 218–236.

Lewis, David E 2003. *Presidents and the Politics of Agency Design: Political Insulation in the United States Government Bureaucracy, 1946–1997*. (Stanford, CA: Stanford University Press).

Lippman, Daniel. 2020. "OPM Chief Dale Cabaniss Abruptly Resigns." *Politico.* (March 17, 2020).

Lipton, Eric. 2020. "Trump Issues Order Giving Him More leeway to Hire and Fire Federal Workers." *The New York Times*, October 22, 2020, https://www.nytimes.com/2020/10/22/us/politics/trump-executive-order-federal-workers.html?referringSource=articleShare

Llorens, Jared J., Donald E. Klingner and John Nalbandian. 2018. *Public Personnel Management: Contexts and Strategies*, seventh edition. (New York: Routledge).

Lloyd–La Follette Act. 1912, P. Law No. 62-336, 37 Stat. 555 (August 24, 1912).

Maranto, Robert. 1998. "Thinking the Unthinkable in Public Administration: A Case for Spoils in the Federal Bureaucracy." *Administration and Society*, Vol. 29, No. 6, pp. 623–642.

Mascott, Jennifer L. 2018. "Who Are 'Officers of the United States?'." *Stanford Law Review*, Vol. 70(February), pp. 443–564.

Meacham, Jon. 2008. *American Lion: Andrew Jackson in the White House*. (New York: Random House).

Meier, Kenneth J. and John Bohte. 2007. *Politics and the Bureaucracy: Policymaking in the Fourth Branch of Government*, fifth edition. (Belmont, CA: Thomson Wadsworth Publishing Company).

Millard, Candice. 2011. *Destiny of the Republic: A Tale of Madness, Medicine, and Murder of a President*. (New York: Doubleday).

Miller, Gary J. and Andrew B. Whitford. 2016. *Above Politics: Bureaucratic Discretion and Credible Commitment*. (New York: Cambridge University Press).

Mitchell, Robert B 2017. *Congress and the King of Frauds: Corruption and the Crédit Mobilier Scandal at the Dawn of the Gilded Age*. (Roseville, Minn: Edinborough Press).

Moran, Sean. 2024. "Is it time to get rid of OPM?" *Government Executive.* (February 23, 2024). Accessed at: https://www.govexec.com/management/2024/02/it-time-get-rid-opm/394327/.

Mosher, Frederick C. 1975. *American Public Administration: Past, Present, Future*, second edition. (Birmingham, AL: University of Alabama Press).

Mosher, Frederick C. 1982. *Democracy and the Public Service*, second edition. (New York: Oxford University Press).

Moynihan, Donald P. 2021. "Public Management for Populists: Trump's Schedule F Executive Order and the Future of the Civil Service." *Public Administration Review*, Vol. 82, No. 1, pp. 174–178.

Muhlhausen, David B., ed. 2017a. *Special Report No. 192, Blueprint for Reorganization: An Analysis of Federal Departments and Agencies*. (Washington, D.C.: The Heritage Foundation). (June 12, 2017).

Muhlhausen, David B., ed. 2017b. *Special Report No. 193, Blueprint for Reorganization: Pathways to Reform and Cross-Cutting Issues*. (Washington, D.C.: The Heritage Foundation). June 30, 2017).

Mulvaney, Mick. 2017. "Memorandum for Heads of Executive Departments and Agencies." Office of Management and Budget, Executive Office of the President, M-17-22. (April 12, 2017).

National Academy of Public Administration. 2021. *Elevating Human Capital: Reframing the U.S. Office of Personnel Management's Leadership Imperative.* (Washington, D.C.: Academy Project Number: 102253, March 2021).

National Archives. 1995. *Records of the Merit Systems Protection Board.* (Record Group 479). Accessed at: https://www.archives.gov/research/guide-fed-records/groups/479.html

National Federation of Federal Employees, Local 1309 v. *Department of the Interior*, 526 U.S. 86 (1999).

National Treasury Employees Unions v. *Federal Labor Relations Authority*, 1 F.4th 1120 (D.C. Cir. June 22, 2021).

Nigro, Lloyd G. and J. Edward Kellough. 2000. "Civil Service Reform in Georgia: Going to the Edge?." *Review of Public Personnel Administration*, Vol. 20, No. 4, pp. 41–54.

Nigro, Lloyd G. and J. Edward Kellough. 2014. *The New Public Personnel Administration*, seventh edition. (Boston, Wadsworth: Cengage Learning).

Ogrysko, Nicole. 2018. "A Member-Less MSPB More Likely as Senate Committee Fails to Clear Pending Nominees." *Federal News Network.* (November 28, 2018). Accessed at: https://federalnewsnetwork.com/all-news/2018/11/a-member-less-mspb-more-likely-as-senate-committee-fails-to-clear-pending-nominees/

Ogrysko, Nicole. 2019a. "Senate Committee Clears 2 Nominees, But for Now Leaves MSPB's Future Hanging by a Thread." *Federal News Network.* (February 13). Accessed at: https://federalnewsnetwork.com/workforce-rightsgovernance/2019/02/senate-committee-clears-2-nominees-but-for-now-leaves-mspbs-future-hanging-by-a-thread/

Ogrysko, Nicole. 2019b. "With No Quick Fix in Sight, MSPB Careening Toward 'Unprecedented' Scenario Thursday." *Federal News Network.* (February 27). Accessed at: https://federalnewsnetwork.com/workforce-rightsgovernance/2019/02/with-no-quick-fix-in-sight-mspb-careening-toward-unprecedented-scenario-thursday/

Ogrysko, Nicole. 2019c. "Trump Nominates Long-Awaited Third MSPB Member." *Federal News Network.* (April 30). Accessed at: https://federalnewsnetwork.com/workforce/2019/04/trump-nominates-long-awaited-third-mspb-member/

Ogrysko, Nicole. 2020. "Lack of Quorum Hits 3-Year Mark, With No Clear End in Sight," *Federal News Network.* (January 24, 2020). Accessed at: https://federalnewsnetwork.com/workforce/2020/01/lack-of-quorum-hits-3-year-mark-at-mspb-with-no-clear-end-in-sight/

Ogrysko, Nicole. 2021a. "Historic Absences at MSPB Hit 4-Year Mark, Creating Potentially Costly Backlog." *Federal News Network.* (January 13, 2021). Accessed at: https://federalnewsnetwork.com/workforce-rightsgovernance/2021/01/historic-absences-at-mspb-hit-4-year-mark-creating-potentially-costly-backlog/

Ogrysko, Nicole. 2021b. "Biden at Last Announces Two MSPB Nominees, Enough to Restore A Quorum." *Federal News Network.* (June 24, 2021). Accessed at: https://federalnewsnetwork.com/people/2021/06/biden-at-last-announces-two-mspb-nominees-enough-to-restore-a-quorum/

Ogrysko, Nicole. 2021c. "After Years of Historic Absences, Biden's MSPB Nominees Face their First Test." *Federal News Network.* (September 22, 2021).Accessed at: https://federalnewsnetwork.com/workforce/2021/09/after-years-of-historic-absences-bidens-mspb-nominees-face-their-first-test/

Ogrysko, Nicole. 2021d. "Schedule F is Gone, But Debate Continues in Congress." *Federal News Network.* (February 24, 2021). Accessed at: https://federalnewsnetwork. com/workforce/2021/02/schedule-f-is-gone-but-the-debate-continues-in-congress/

Rainey, Hal G. 1997. "The 'How Much Process is Due?' Debate: Legal and Managerial Perspectives." in P. J. Cooper and C. A. Newland, eds. *Handbook of Public Law and Administration.* (San Francisco: Jossey-Bass Publishers).

Reardon, Anthony M. (NTEU National President). 2021. "Memorandum to Chapter Presidents." (June 22, 2021).

Rein, Lisa. 2020. "Federal Personnel Chief Quits Abruptly Amid Coronavirus Planning for the Workforce of 2.1 Million." *The Washington Post.* (March 17, 2020).

Relyea, Harold C 2008. *Presidential Directives: Background and Overview.* (Washington, D.C.: Congressional Research Service).

Riccucci, Norma M., Katherine C. Naff and Madinah F. Hamidullah. 2020. *Personnel Management in Government: Politics and Process*, eighth edition. (New York: Routledge, Taylor & Francis Group).

Rockman, Bert A. 2019. "Bureaucracy Between Populism and Technocracy." *Administration and Society*, Vol. 51, No. 10, pp. 1546–1575.

Rourke, Francis E 1965. *Bureaucratic Power in National Politics.* (Boston: Little, Brown, and Company).

Rourke, Francis E 1984. *Bureaucracy, Politics, and Public Policy, third edition.* (Boston: Little, Brown, and Company).

Rucker, Philip and Robert Costa. 2017. "Bannon Vows a Daily Fight for 'Deconstruction of the Administrative State.' *The Washington Post*, (February 23, 2017). Accessed at: https://www.washingtonpost.com/politics/top-wh-strategist-vows-a-daily-fight-for-deconstruction-of-the-administrative-state/2017/02/23/03f6b8da-f9ea-11e6-bf01-d47f8cf9b643_story.html

Samuels, Brett and Zack Budryk. 2020. "OPM Chief Abruptly Resigns." *The Hill.* (March 17, 2020). Accessed at: https://thehill.com/homenews/administration/488129-opm-chief-abruptly-resigns-report/

Sherk, James. 2021. "Increasing Accountability in the Civil Service." America First Policy Institute. (May 26, 2021). Accessed at: https://americafirstpolicy.com/latest/increasing-accountability-in-the-civil-service

Sherk, James. 2022. "Tales from the Swamp: How Federal Bureaucrats Resisted President Trump." America First Policy Institute. (February 1, 2022).Accessed at: https://americafirstpolicy.com/latest/20222702-federal-bureaucrats-resisted-president-trump

Shimabukuro, Jon O. and Jennifer A. Staman. 2019. *Categories of Federal Civil S ervice Employment: A Snapshot.* (Washington D.C.: Congressional Research Service). (March 26, 2019). Accessed at: https://www.everycrsreport.com/files/20190326_R45635_9fbe73a53a2c42612b670dcff44500be63ded82e.pdf

Shugerman, J. (2020). *The Imaginary Unitary Executive*. Lawfare. Retrieved February 8, 2023, from https://www.lawfareblog.com/imaginary-unitary-executive

Simon, Herbert A 1947. *Administrative Behavior: A Study of Decision-Making Processes in Administrative Organization*. (New York: Macmillan).

Skowronek, Stephen. 2009. "The Conservative Insurgency and Presidential Power: A Developmental Perspective on the Unitary Executive." *Harvard Law Review*, Vol. 122, No. 8, pp. 2070–2103.

Skowronek, Stephen, John A. Dearborn and Desmond King 2021. *Phantoms of a Beleaguered Republic: The Deep State and the Unitary Executive*. (New York: Oxford University Press).

Smith, Ralph R. 2021. "Political Donations and Federal Employees in 2020 Elections." FedSmith.com. (February 12, 2021). Accessed at: https://www.fedsmith.com/2021/02/12/political-donations-and-federal-employees/

Smith, Ralph R. 2022. "A Zipper Clause: Why Agencies and Unions Fight Over it." FedSmith.com. (January 29, 2022). Accessed at: https://www.fedsmith.com/2022/01/28/zipper-clause-why-agenecies-unions-fight-over-it/

Stein, Jeff and Jacob Bogage. 2024. "Trump Plans to Claim Sweeping Powers to Cancel Federal Spending." *The Washington Post*. (June 7, 2024). Accessed at: https://www.washingtonpost.com/business/2024/06/07/trump-budget-impoundment-congress/#

Swan, Jonathan. 2022a. "Inside Trump 25: A Radical Plan for Trump's Second Term." Axios. (July 22, 2022). Accessed at: https://www.axios.com/2022/07/22/trump-2025-radical-plan-second-term

Swan, Jonathan. 2022b. "Inside Trump 25: Trump's Revenge." Axios. (July 22, 2022). Accessed at: https://www.axios.com/2022/07/23/donald-trump-news-schedule-f-executive-order

U.S. Civil Service Commission. 1904. *Twentieth Annual Report of the United States Civil Service Commission, July 1, 1902 to June 30, 1903*. (Washington, D.C.: Government Printing Office, 1904), p. 62.

U.S. Congress. 1978a. *Civil Service Reform Act of 1978*. Title II, Section 201(a). (Public Law No. 92-454, 92 Stat. 1119).

U.S. Congress. 1978b. *Civil Service Reform Act of 1978*. Title VII. (Public Law No. 92-454, 92 Stat. 1200).

U.S. Congress. 2019. *National Defense Authorization Act for Fiscal Year 2020*. (Public Law No. 116-92, 133 Stat. 1601–1603).

U.S. House of Representatives. 2019a. Hearing Before the Subcommittee on Government Operations, Committee on Oversight and Reform 116 Congress, First Session, Serial No. 116-26, May 21, 2019, "The Administration's War on a Merit-Based Civil Service." (Washington, D.C.: Government Publishing Office).

U.S. House of Representatives. 2019b. Hearing Before the Subcommittee on Government Operations, Committee on Oversight and Reform 116 Congress, First Session, Serial No. 116-33, June 4, 2019, "Examining Federal Labor-Management Relations." (Washington, D.C.: Government Publishing Office).

U.S. Merit Systems Protection Board. 2015. *What Is Due Process in Federal Employment? A Report to the President and Congress of the United States*. (May 2015).

Accessed at: https://www.mspb.gov/studies/studies/What_is_Due_Process_in_Federal_ Civil_Service_Employment_1166935.pdf

U.S. Merit Systems Protection Board. 2017. *Annual Report for FY 2016.* (January 18). Accessed at: https://www.mspb.gov/about/annual_reports/MSPB_FY_2016_Annual_ Report_1374269.pdf

U.S. Merit Systems Protection Board. 2022a. *Annual Report for FY 2021.* (February 18). Accessed at: https://www.mspb.gov/about/annual_reports/MSPB_FY_2021_Annual_ Report_1900943.pdf

U.S. Merit Systems Protection Board. 2022b. "Recent Board Members." Accessed at: https://www.mspb.gov/about/recentmembers.htm

U.S. Merit Systems Protection Board. 2022c. "Board Members." Accessed at: https:// www.mspb.gov/about/members.htm

U.S. Merit Systems Protection Board. 2022d. "Board Members' Service." (January 1979– March 2022). Accessed at: https://www.mspb.gov/about/BoardTermsChartMarch2022.pdf

U.S. Government Accountability Office. 2022. *Civil Service: Agency Responses and Perspectives on Former Executive Order to Create a New Schedule F Category of Federal Positions.* (GAO – 2222 – 110055550044; September 28, 2022).

U.S. Office of Management and Budget. 2018. "Delivering Government Solutions in the 21st Century: Reform Plan and Reorganization Recommendations." Executive Office of the President. (June 21, 2018).

U.S. Office of Management and Budget. 2019. "Administrative Services Merger Act of 2019." Executive Office of the President. (May 16, 2019). Accessed at: https://cdn. govexec.com/media/gbc/docs/pdfs_edit/051619ew1.pdf

U.S. Office of Personnel Management. 2018 "Excepted Service Hiring Authorities: Their Use and Effectiveness in the Executive Branch." (July 2018). Accessed at: https:// www.opm.gov/policy-data-oversight/hiring-information/excepted-service/excepted- service-study-report.pdf

U.S. Office of Personnel Management. 2019. "OPM Reorganization." Accessed at: https:// federalnewsnetwork.com/wp-content/uploads/2019/05/CASE-FOR-CHANGE.pdf

U.S. Senate. 2017. Hearing before the Committee on Homeland Security and Gov- ernmental Affairs. 115th Congress, First Session. November 7, 2017. (Washington, D.C.: U.S. Government Publishing Office). Accessed at: https://www.congress.gov/ event/115th-congress/senate-event/LC62322/text

U.S. Senate. 2018a. Hearing before the Committee on Homeland Security and Govern- mental Affairs. 115th Congress, Second Session. July 19, 2018. (Washington, D.C.: U.S. Government Publishing Office). Accessed at: https://www.govinfo.gov/content/ pkg/CHRG-115shrg32490/pdf/CHRG-115shrg32490.pdf

U.S. Senate. 2018b. Committee on Homeland Security and Governmental Affairs. 115th Con- gress, Second Session. November 28, 2018. *Committee Record 11-28-2018.* Accessed at: https://www.hsgac.senate.gov/imo/media/doc/Committee%20Record-2018-11-28.pdf

U.S. Senate. 2019a. Committee on Homeland Security and Governmental Affairs. 116th Congress, First Session. February 13, 2019. *Committee Record 02-13-2019.* Ac- cessed at: https://www.hsgac.senate.gov/imo/media/doc/Committee%20Record- 2019-02-13.pdf

U.S. Senate. 2019b. Hearing before the Committee on Homeland Security and Governmental Affairs. 116ᵗʰ Congress, First Session. June 12, 2019. (Washington, D.C.: U.S. Government Publishing Office). Accessed at: https://www.congress.gov/event/116th-congress/senate-event/LC64287/text?s=1&r=1

U.S. Senate. 2019c. Committee on Homeland Security and Governmental Affairs. 116ᵗʰ Congress, First Session. February 13, 2019. *Committee Record 06-19-2019*. Accessed at: https://www.hsgac.senate.gov/imo/media/doc/Committee%20Record-2019-06-191.pdf

U.S. Senate. 2019d. Hearing before the Committee on Homeland Security and Governmental Affairs. 116ᵗʰ Congress, First Session. July 16, 2019. (Washington, D.C.: U.S. Government Publishing Office). Accessed at: https://www.congress.gov/event/116th-congress/senate-event/LC64350/text

U.S. Senate. 2021. Hearing before the Committee on Homeland Security and Governmental Affairs. 117ᵗʰ Congress, First Session. September 22, 2021. Accessed at: https://www.hsgac.senate.gov/hearings/nominations-of-cathy-a-harris-to-be-a-member-and-chair-and-tristan-l-leavitt-and-raymond-a-limon-to-be-members-merit-systems-protection-board

U.S. Senate. 2022. Committee on Homeland Security and Governmental Affairs. 117ᵗʰ Congress, Second Session. Nominations. Accessed at: https://www.hsgac.senate.gov/nominations

Van Riper, P Paul. 1958. *History of the United States Civil Service*. (Evanston, IL: Row, Peterson and Company).

Wagner, Erich. 2017. "Union Official Blasts Lack of Ideological Diversity on Mediation Panel." *Government Executive*. (August 22, 2017). Accessed at: https://www.govexec.com/management/2017/08/union-official-blasts-lack-ideological-diversity-mediation-panel/140428/

Wagner, Erich. 2019a. "Labor-Management Impasse Panel Guts Telework, Holiday Leave for Some Feds." *Government Executive*. (April 5, 2019). Accessed at: https://www.govexec.com/management/2019/04/labor-management-impasse-panel-guts-telework-holiday-leave-some-feds/156117/

Wagner, Erich. 2019b. "White House's OPM-GSA Merger Bill Gives an Unconfirmed Appointee Authority over Personnel Rules." *Government Executive*. (May 16, 2019). Accessed at: https://www.govexec.com/management/2019/05/white-houses-opm-gsa-merger-bill-gives-unconfirmed-appointee-authority-over-personnel-rules/157085/

Wagner, Erich. 2019c. "Impasses Panel Guts Telework, Official Time for Employees at Social Security Administration." *Government Executive*. (June 3, 2019). Accessed at: https://www.govexec.com/management/2019/06/impasses-panel-guts-telework-official-time-employees-social-security-administration/157448/

Wagner, Erich. 2019d. "House Appropriations Bill Would Block Impasses Panel from Imposing New Union Contracts." *Government Executive*. (July 2, 2019). Accessed at: https://www.govexec.com/management/2019/07/house-appropriations-bill-would-block-impasses-panel-imposing-new-union-contracts/158172/

Wagner, Erich. 2020. "OPM Quietly Abandons Proposed Merger with GSA." *Government Executive.* (October 30, 2020). Accessed at: https://www.govexec.com/management/2020/10/opm-quietly-abandons-proposed-merger-gsa/169692/print/

Wagner, Erich. 2021. "Biden Names Acting FLRA General Counsel, Ending Critical Trump Era Vacancy." *Government Executive.* (March 24, 2021). Accessed at: https://www.govexec.com/management/2021/03/biden-names-acting-flra-general-counsel-ending-critical-trump-era-vacancy/172903/

Wagner, Erich. 2022a. "Trump is Threatening the Return and Expansion of Schedule F." *Government Executive.* (March 14, 2022). Accessed at: https://www.govexec.com/workforce/2022/03/trump-threatening-return-and-expansion-schedule-f/363145/

Wagner, Erich. 2022b. "Some House Republicans Want to Reinstall Trump Workforce Policies." *Government Executive.* (March 17, 2022). Accessed at: https://www.govexec.com/workforce/2022/03/some-house-republicans-want-reinstall-trump-workforce-policies/363311/

Wagner, Erich. 2022c. "The House Has Approved a Bill to Prevent Future Schedules F." *Government Executive* (September 15, 2022). Accessed at: https://www.govexec.com/workforce/2022/09/house-has-approved-bill-prevent-future-schedules-f/377219/

Wagner, Erich. 2023. "VA, AFGE Celebrate 'Best Union Contract' in Federal Government." Government Executive (August 8, 2023). Accessed at: https://www.govexec.com/workforce/2023/08/va-afge-celebrate-best-union-contract-federal-government/389228/

Waldo, Dwight 1948. *The Administrative State.* (New York: The Ronald Press Company).

Walker, David M. 2003. *Executive Reorganization Authority: Balancing Executive and Congressional Roles in Shaping the Federal Government's Structure.* (Washington, D.C.: General Accounting Office).

White, Leonard D. 1956. *The Federalists: A Study in Administrative History.* (New York: The Macmillan Co, second printing).

White, Leonard D. 1951. *The Jeffersonians: A Study in Administrative History 1801–1829.* (New York: The Macmillan Co).

White, Leonard D. 1954. *The Jacksonians: A Study in Administrative History 1829–1861.* (New York: The Macmillan Co).

White, Leonard D. 1958. *The Republican Era: A Study in Administrative History 1869–1901.* (New York: The Macmillan Co).

Yoder, Eric and Lisa Rein. 2018. "Trump Abruptly Replaces Federal Personnel Director After Just 7 Months." *The Washington Post.* (October 5, 2018). Accessed at: https://www.washingtonpost.com/politics/trump-abruptly-replaces-federal-personnel-director-after-just-7-months/2018/10/05/29497f6e-c8dd-11e8-b1ed-1d2d65b86d0c_story.html

INDEX

Note: Page numbers in **bold** refer to tables.

Printed in the United States
by Baker & Taylor Publisher Services